NO LONGER PROPERTY OF
SEATTLE PUBLIC LIBRARY

University of Utah

OCT 05 2009

SCIENCE
FOUNDATIONS

Natural Selection

SCIENCE FOUNDATIONS

SCIENCE
FOUNDATIONS

Natural Selection

J. PHIL GIBSON AND TERRI R. GIBSON

CHELSEA HOUSE
PUBLISHERS
An imprint of Infobase Publishing

Natural Selection

Copyright © 2009 by Infobase Publishing

All rights reserved. No part of this book may be reproduced or utilized in any form or by any means, electronic or mechanical, including photocopying, recording, or by any information storage or retrieval systems, without permission in writing from the publisher. For information, contact:

Chelsea House
An imprint of Infobase Publishing
132 West 31st Street
New York NY 10001

Library of Congress Cataloging-in-Publication Data
Gibson, J. Phil.
  Natural selection / J. Phil Gibson and Terri R. Gibson.
      p. cm. — (Science foundations)
  Includes bibliographical references and index.
  ISBN 978-0-7910-9784-7 (hardcover)
  1. Natural selection. 2. Evolution (Biology) I. Gibson, Terri R. II. Title.
III. Series.
  QH375.G53 2009
  576.8'2—dc22   2008047252

Chelsea House books are available at special discounts when purchased in bulk quantities for businesses, associations, institutions, or sales promotions. Please call our Special Sales Department in New York at (212) 967-8800 or (800) 322-8755.

You can find Chelsea House on the World Wide Web at

http://www.chelseahouse.com

Text design by Kerry Casey

Cover design by Ben Peterson

Printed in the United States of America

Bang EJB 10 9 8 7 6 5 4 3 2 1

This book is printed on acid-free paper.

All links and Web addresses were checked and verified to be correct at the time of publication. Because of the dynamic nature of the Web, some addresses and links may have changed since publication and may no longer be valid.

Contents

Adaptation

From so simple a beginning endless forms most beautiful and most wonderful have been, and are being, evolved.
—Charles Darwin, *The Origin of Species*

The cobra lily (*Darlingtonia californica*) lurks in the bogs and marshes of northern California and southern Oregon, as deadly, in its own way, as its reptilian namesake. The hood, which gives the cobra lily its name, attracts unsuspecting insects with sweet-smelling nectar. An insect crawling under the hood to feed on the nectar finds itself in a vertical tube formed by the plant's leaves. Thin areas in the hood act as tiny windows, allowing light into the tube. When the insect has eaten its fill, it flies toward the light. Instead of escaping into the open air, however, it bumps into the slick, waxy surface of the hood, and then falls into the liquid at the bottom of the tube. Unable to fly with wet wings, the insect attempts to climb the walls of the tube. Unfortunately for the insect, hundreds of sharp, downward-pointing hairs lining the tube make climbing out impossible. The insect falls into the liquid for the last time, where it is slowly digested in a mixture of rainwater and mildly acidic juices produced by the cobra lily.

Why would a plant need to eat insects? Why would it produce a hood with nectar and tiny windows? How did it start to make the

Figure 1.1 The cobra lily (*Darlingtonia californica*) is a carnivorous plant found in California and Oregon.

curved hairs? The answer is survival. Like all living things, plants need nutrients to live. Most plants get their nutrients from the soil in which they grow. The soil in bogs, however, is generally low in nutrients. Carnivorous plants such as the cobra lily obtain the nutrients they need by trapping insects, dissolving their body parts, and absorbing the nutrients. The windows and nectar are traits that work as part of the trap the plant uses to lure its insect meals.

Not all insects that visit the cobra lily become its victims. Some insects actually use this plant as their home. The pitcher plant mosquito (*Wyeomyia smithii*) and the slime mite (*Sarraceniopus darlingtoniae)* lay their eggs in the plant's digestive juices. The mosquito and mite larvae thrive in the liquid, feasting on the remains of trapped insects until they mature and are able to leave the tube and lay their own eggs in another cobra lily leaf. These insects have unique traits that allow them to tolerate the deadly conditions inside a cobra lily leaf, living in a place that most insects would probably rather not visit.

ADAPTATIONS

The special traits that the cobra lily, pitcher plant mosquito, and slime mite use to survive are examples of **adaptations**. An adaptation is any structural, behavioral, or physiological feature that helps an organism survive in its **environment**. Throughout history, different human cultures have arrived at a variety of explanations for their observations of the natural world in general and for the adaptations of organisms in particular. While these explanations can have tremendous cultural and personal value, they do not provide biologists with a strong scientific basis for understanding the origins and value of adaptations in the natural world.

In addition to studying adaptations in living organisms, biologists also examine **fossils** (the remains or impressions of organisms from previous geological ages). The similarities and differences between present and past life-forms on Earth help scientists understand adaptations. For example, fossils of dinosaurs show similarities with modern alligators (*Alligator mississippiensis*) and crocodiles (*Crocodylus* species). These similarities help biologists understand the origins of alligators and crocodiles as well as how life on Earth has changed and how important adaptations have evolved. In the past, these observations led biologists to ask whether any natural

Figure 1.2   Charles Darwin in 1874

forces or processes could be identified to explain the many amazing changes and adaptations that the fossils revealed.

Many scientists began to investigate these questions. From their observations and experiments, they developed different ideas about how adaptations arise and change over time. It was not until a young English biologist named Charles Darwin investigated the topics of change, adaptation, and **species**, however, that the force driving the origin of adaptations and species was identified. Darwin called this force **natural selection**.

Natural selection is an important biological principle that is often misunderstood and misinterpreted. Very simply, natural selection is the process through which some individuals of a species have traits (adaptations) that allow them to survive and produce more offspring than other individuals of their species. Consequently, the traits that

Lamarck

Jean-Baptiste Pierre Antoine de Monet, Chevalier de Lamarck, was a French biologist who proposed a theory called inheritance of acquired characteristics. In his theory, parents acquired traits throughout their lives that they passed on to their offspring. Giraffes (*Giraffa camelopardalis*), for example, are thought to have originally had short necks. According to Lamarck, giraffes that stretched their necks to reach high leaves actually made their necks longer and produced offspring that had longer necks than their parents did when they were born. Similarly, a blacksmith who develops strong muscles while working at his forge should have stronger children than a poet who flexes his brain more often than his biceps. Biologists tested this idea by cutting the tails off mice and other animals, and then allowing them to breed. In contrast to expectations from Lamarck's theory, the offspring of tailless adults always had tails. Thus, although his theory was wrong, it could be tested scientifically to determine its validity.

help them survive and leave more descendants become more common. Natural selection is often confused with **evolution**, which is the change in a species over time, but natural selection and evolution are not the same thing. Natural selection is one of several different processes that can cause evolutionary change. Natural selection, however, is the only evolutionary process that can result in adaptations that help organisms survive in their environment.

THE SCIENTIFIC METHOD AND SCIENTIFIC THEORIES

The word *science* comes from the Latin term *scientia*, which means "to know." Science is exactly that, a way of investigating and knowing about the natural world. When scientists investigate questions, they cannot accept an explanation for an observation of the natural world simply because it makes a good story. Instead, they use an approach called the **scientific method** to investigate the natural world systematically. The scientific method can be used to answer questions ranging from why chemicals react in certain ways to how adaptations function.

The scientific method is composed of several steps. First, an observation is made. For example, one might notice that some plants produce more seeds than others do, and plants that produce more seeds also produce flowers that attract more butterflies. Second, a question is asked that may explain the observation—in this case, "Do the flowers that attract more butterflies produce more nectar than flowers that attract fewer butterflies?" Third, a possible explanation, or **hypothesis**, for the observation is developed—for example, "If different flowers make different amounts of nectar, then plants that make more nectar should attract more butterflies, be pollinated more often, and consequently produce more seeds." This hypothesis not only makes a statement about the observation, but also makes a *testable* prediction to explain how it might work.

The next step gets to the heart of science, which is to design and conduct an experiment. In the example above, an experiment

Naming Species

Different organisms are known by different names. The names familiar to most people are common names, such as dog, oak, or catfish, that are used by people in daily conversation. Scientists, however, identify species using a system developed by the Swedish naturalist Carl Linné, who was also known as Carolus Linnaeus (1707–1778). He developed a system in which each species is given a two-part scientific name called a **binomial**. For example, the scientific name for humans is *Homo sapiens*. The first part of the name, *Homo* (meaning "man"), is the **genus**, while the second part, *sapiens* (meaning "wise"), is the species, sometimes called the **epithet**. Together, the genus and epithet constitute a complete scientific name of a species. Other species in the same genus are given a different epithet. For example, the now-extinct Neanderthal is known as *Homo neanderthalensis* (meaning "Neanderthal man"). When scientists want to refer to all the different species in a genus, they follow the genus name with "spp." For example, the scientific name *Pinus pungens* refers only to a specific species, the table mountain pine, while *Pinus* spp. refers collectively to all species in the pine genus *Pinus*.

could measure the amount of nectar produced by different flowers and count the number of butterfly visitors. Another way to conduct the experiment would be to add or remove nectar from flowers to determine whether this affects butterfly visits and seed production. Once the experiment is complete, the scientist analyzes the information, or **data**, collected during the experiment and interprets the results in light of the hypothesis. If, in this example, significantly more butterflies visited high-nectar-producing plants than low-nectar-producing plants, a biologist could conclude that nectar levels help determine how many butterflies visit a flower. If those flowers also produce more seeds, a biologist could conclude that plants with more nectar will produce more offspring. If the results of the experiment showed no significant differences in butterfly visitation or seed production between plants with high and low nectar levels, however, a new hypothesis would have to be developed and tested.

For the results of any experiment to be scientifically acceptable, they must be repeatable, and they must suggest explanations that can be investigated further by other scientists. The scientific method can use only testable natural forces to explain observations and experimental results. This is particularly important for scientific studies of adaptations. As mentioned previously, different cultures have proposed a variety of explanations for the diversity of life on Earth and the many adaptations observed. Science, however, can consider only those explanations that have a basis in observable natural processes.

Eventually, after numerous tests, a particular observation may become so well established that it is considered a fact and there is no need for further testing. For example, many independent experiments conducted on different species could show that butterflies do

Scientific Theories

Theories are a critical part of science. They provide a comprehensive explanation for observed phenomena and known facts. For example, much of what is known about chemistry is based upon atomic theory, which states that all matter is composed of atoms that have specific measurable properties. The general theory of relativity describes the force of gravity. Although these two theories provide conceptual foundations of chemistry and physics, respectively, they are still open to further testing through experimentation. If the results of different experiments do not meet the predictions of a theory, the theory can be modified to explain the new data. This important aspect of scientific theories allows scientists to ask questions and develop experiments, thereby advancing our understanding of the natural world.

indeed prefer flowers that produce more nectar over those that produce less. Once a large, well-established body of evidence has been collected to provide an explanation for an observed phenomenon, the facts can be used to develop a **scientific theory**.

A scientific theory is not just a well-founded explanation of natural phenomena or observations. It can also serve as a powerful tool for making predictions regarding related aspects of nature. Using the theory of evolution, the observation of an evolutionary change in the **lineage** of an organism suggests that an environmental source of natural selection and some degree of natural variation in one or more traits of the organism should be detectable after closer study.

It is important to recognize that the word *theory* has a very different meaning to scientists than it does to the general public. In common usage, *theory* means a speculation or guess. To a scientist, however, a scientific theory is not a guess. The scientific meaning of *theory* refers to an all-encompassing explanation of many well-supported observations and facts that explain a natural phenomenon. As with any other aspect of science, a theory can be revised and expanded based upon the introduction of new data.

The attempt to discredit the theory of evolution by natural selection with the argument that it is "just a theory" wrongly assumes that scientists use the word *theory* as a synonym for *guess*. Natural selection and evolution are sound scientific theories supported by a tremendous amount of data that provide an explanation for many adaptations observed in many different species. Such well-established theories can be considered facts.

SUMMARY

Living things possess traits that help them survive in their environment. These traits are called adaptations. While many explanations have been developed to propose the origin of adaptations, biologists have shown that a process discovered by Charles Darwin called natural selection is the force that drives the evolution of adaptations. Through the scientific method, scientists have confirmed that natural selection is the important natural process that acts on all living things and produces adaptation.

Charles Darwin

There is grandeur in this view of life.
—*Charles Darwin,* The Origin of Species

Twenty-two-year-old Charles Darwin stood on the deck of the HMS *Beagle* as it sailed from Devonport, England, on December 27, 1831. The *Beagle*, a 10-gun brig commanded by Captain Robert FitzRoy of the Royal Navy, had been commissioned to survey and map the South American continent and a series of islands in the Pacific Ocean. It would be Darwin's responsibility to collect rocks, fossils, plants, and animals from these exotic locations. With these specimens and his own observations, Darwin would formulate one of the great unifying principles of biology. In his book *The Voyage of the* Beagle, Darwin would write that the beginning of the expedition marked "the first of many delightful days never to be forgotten." Darwin's experiences of the next four years, nine months, and five days would forever alter our understanding of the world around us.

EARLY LIFE

Charles Robert Darwin was born on February 12, 1809, in Shrewsbury, England. He was the fifth of six children born to Robert

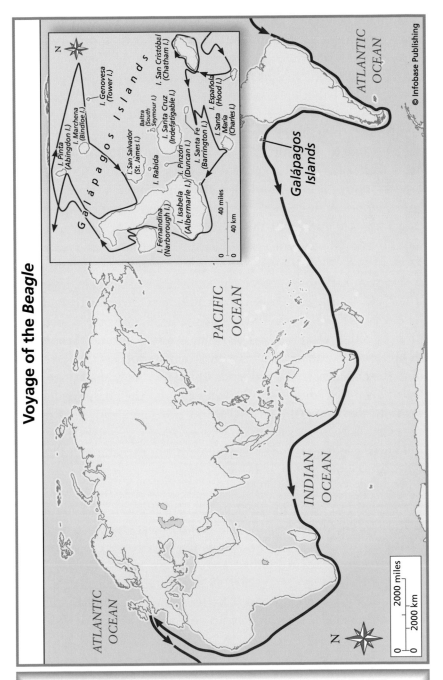

Voyage of the Beagle

Galápagos Islands

Inset labels:

Galápagos Islands

I. Genovesa (Tower I.)

I. Marchena (Bindloe I.)

I. San Cristóbal (Chatham I.)

I. Pinta (Abingdon I.)

Baltra (South Seymour I.)

I. Santa Cruz (Indefatigable I.)

I. Española (Hood I.)

I. San Salvador (St. James I.)

I. Santa María (Charles I.)

I. Rabida

I. Pinzón (Duncan I.)

I. Santa Fe (Barrington I.)

I. Fernandina (Narborough I.)

I. Isabela (Albemarle I.)

40 miles

40 km

PACIFIC OCEAN

ATLANTIC OCEAN

INDIAN OCEAN

ATLANTIC OCEAN

2000 miles

2000 km

N

© Infobase Publishing

Figure 2.1 When he was 22 years old, Charles Darwin set sail on the HMS *Beagle* as the ship's naturalist. It sailed around the world, and included stops at the Galápagos Islands (*inset*), where Darwin made many of the observations that led him to develop his theory of natural selection.

Darwin, a well-known physician, and Susannah Darwin, a member of the prominent Wedgwood family, famous for their pottery.

As a child, Darwin enjoyed the privileges of the upper class. He spent his days outdoors playing sports and studying nature. When he was 16, his father enrolled him in Edinburgh University to study medicine as his grandfather, father, and brother had done. Unlike his family before him, however, Darwin disliked medicine, particularly when it came to dissecting cadavers. What he did enjoy was taking walks with some of his favorite professors, including the zoologist Robert Grant. During these walks, Darwin examined the plants and animals found in the Scottish countryside and along the coast and waterways. He also spent many hours studying the plant and animal collections at the university museum. It was at the museum that Darwin learned how to prepare and preserve specimens.

Darwin's father was upset by his son's lack of interest in medicine. In 1827, he transferred Darwin to Cambridge University to study for the clergy. Again, Darwin ignored his father's wishes. He spent his time collecting beetles, a passion that would continue throughout his life. He also attended lectures by scientists such as the Reverend John Stevens Henslow, a professor of botany. As he had done with Robert Grant at Edinburgh, Darwin explored the countryside with Henslow, discussing the natural world and science. Over the next few years, Darwin would befriend many other prominent botanists, zoologists, geologists, and chemists, all of whom fostered his appreciation of science.

It was his friend Henslow who informed Darwin of the three-year expedition being planned by the Royal Navy. The naturalist position was open because the person originally chosen to fill it had declined. For Charles Darwin, it was the opportunity of a lifetime. Unfortunately, Darwin's father was strongly opposed to his son's joining the *Beagle*'s crew. Only after discussing the matter with Josiah and Emma Wedgwood (Charles's uncle and cousin, respectively) did the elder Darwin give his son permission to serve as the *Beagle*'s naturalist.

THE EXPEDITION

Darwin was amazed by the plants and animals he discovered at every new island and forest he explored. He also found many

Figure 2.2 The extinct *Glyptodon* (a large, armadillo-like creature) and *Megatherium* (a giant ground sloth) were significantly larger than the armadillos and sloths we see today.

fossils of extinct creatures that were unknown to science at the time. One particularly important find was the fossilized remains of a species of **glyptodont**. This extinct organism was a giant ancestor of modern armadillos (*Dasypus* spp.). Darwin noted the similarities between existing species and the fossils of extinct, giant animals. Could the features of modern organisms have changed from those of larger, now-extinct ancestors? Unable to answer this question at the time, Darwin shipped many of these fossils and other specimens back to scientists in England for further study.

During the voyage, Darwin read *Principles of Geology* by the eminent geologist Sir Charles Lyell. In this book, Lyell described

Stranger than Fiction

The Galápagos Islands are famous not only for their association with Darwin, but also as the setting for a novel by the great American writer Kurt Vonnegut (1922–2007). In *Galápagos*, Vonnegut weaves the principles of natural selection and evolution into a science-fiction tale in which the last humans on Earth become stranded on the Galápagos Islands. The characters evolve traits that help them survive their harsh environment. Despite being a work of fiction, the story accurately demonstrates how genetic variation and natural selection work together to change species.

how geological phenomena are the result of slow-acting processes that continue to act in the present as they have in the past. According to Lyell, geologic forces could cause layers of rock to raise and lower over time. This concept helped Darwin understand how a layer of shells and other marine organisms could be found in rocky cliffs many feet above the current sea level. After experiencing an earthquake in the town of Valvidia on the Chronos Islands, Darwin saw that some of the rock layers had been lifted several feet above their previous level. These observations allowed Darwin to confirm some of Lyell's ideas about the dynamic nature of the Earth.

On September 15, 1835, Darwin arrived at the place that will forever be tied to his name: the Galápagos Islands. Darwin would later write in *The Voyage of the* Beagle, "The natural history of these islands is eminently curious, and well deserves attention." The Galápagos Islands are an **archipelago**, a chain of 13 volcanic islands, 6 small islands, and 107 islets. They lie on the equator approximately 600 miles (966 kilometers) west of Ecuador in South America. The oldest islands in the archipelago are estimated to be 5 million to 10 million years old. The name *Galápagos* comes from the Spanish word for saddle, *galápago*, which refers to the saddle-shaped shells of some of the giant tortoises found on the islands. These tortoises would play an important role in the development of Darwin's evolutionary theories.

The Galápagos Tortoises Today

From the seventeenth through the nineteenth centuries, sailors caught giant tortoises and kept them alive as a source of fresh meat aboard ships by placing the tortoises

(continues)

Figure 2.3 This saddleback Galápagos tortoise (*Geochelone elephantopus hoodensis*) is feeding on arid vegetation on Pinzon Island on the Galápagos Islands west of Ecuador. Saddleback tortoises live on drier islands where the vegetation grows taller than in wetter areas. The saddle-backed tortoise's longer neck and arched shell allow it to feed in these areas.

(continued)

on their backs. This barbaric practice almost drove the species to extinction, because the turtles most often collected were females captured during the egg-laying process. Rats, goats, pigs, and other animals introduced to the Galápagos by the sailors also decreased the turtle populations by eating their eggs and damaging their nests. Efforts to protect the Galápagos tortoise populations began in the 1960s. Since that time, their numbers have rebounded.

Scientists have determined that there were once 15 subspecies of giant Galápagos tortoises. Four of the subspecies are now extinct. One subspecies from the island of Pinta had been reduced to a single male named "Lonesome George." Scientists, however, recently discovered a group of tortoises that may contain members of the same subspecies. If so, it may be possible to preserve this subspecies, turning the story of Lonesome George from an extinction tragedy to a conservation success.

The Galápagos Tortoises

All of the Galápagos tortoises are members of the species *Geochelone elephantopus*. They are similar to tortoises found in South America except for their tremendous size. They can weigh as much as 700 pounds (317.5 kilograms). Their shells alone can reach up to 4 feet (1.2 meters) in length. There are 15 recognized **races** or **subspecies** of the Galápagos tortoise. Four of these have become extinct since Darwin's time.

When Darwin arrived at the islands, he learned to identify which island a tortoise was from simply by looking at its shell. Tortoises from islands with lush, low-growing vegetation have dome-shaped shells, while tortoises from islands with mostly shrubby vegetation have saddle-shaped shells that form an arch over the neck. Tortoises with arched shells are able to raise their necks higher. This allows them to feed on the higher-growing vegetation of their islands. Darwin also noticed that dome-shelled tortoises were larger and lived on cooler, wetter islands. The saddle-shelled tortoises were smaller and lived on the warmer, drier islands.

The Galápagos Finches

The birds on the islands also gave Darwin much to think about. Initially, he thought the small, drab, brown or black birds that inhabited the different islands in the archipelago were different kinds of mockingbirds, finches, and wrens because of their dramatically different beaks. The various sizes and shapes of beaks allowed them to eat different seeds, fruits, and insects. Much to Darwin's astonishment, two species of bird even used cactus spines to probe rotting wood for grubs and other insects.

While Darwin noted that these birds were similar to certain species he had observed in South America, he did not fully realize the importance of this fact at the time. As before, he collected specimens to take to England for further study.

In addition to the tortoises and finches, Darwin noted how well-suited other species are to life in the harsh environment of the

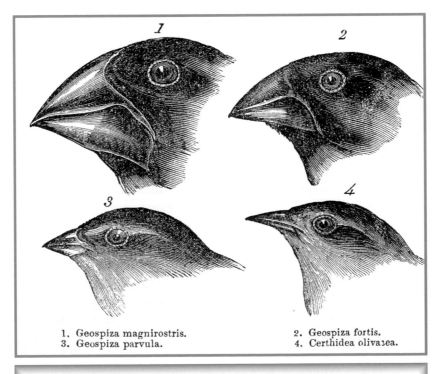

1. Geospiza magnirostris.
2. Geospiza fortis.
3. Geospiza parvula.
4. Certhidea olivaɔea.

Figure 2.4   The four distinct beaks seen on these Galápagos finches helped Charles Darwin develop his idea of natural selection. This drawing comes from Darwin's *A Naturalist's Voyage Round the World.*

Galápagos. The two species of land iguana present, *Conolophus subcristatus* and *Conolophus pallidus*, show characteristics that allow them to live and feed on land. The other lizard species present, the marine iguana *Amblyrhynchus cristatus*, has slightly different traits that allow it to feed on algae in the ocean and live on the rocky shores of the island. Plants, too, show specializations similar to what Darwin observed in animals. One group of plants in particular, the tree daisies (*Scalesia* spp.), show unique adaptations and specializations for growth on different islands. The unique features of the different tree daisy species are suited to growth in specific environmental conditions, making them the botanical equivalent to Darwin's finches.

Return to England

The HMS *Beagle* left the Galápagos on October 20, 1835. The expedition visited several other locations, including Tahiti, New Zealand, Australia, and Africa. The ship eventually docked almost a year later at Falmouth, England, on October 2, 1836. Darwin bade farewell to Captain FitzRoy and the crew and returned home to begin thinking about what he had observed on his amazing, life-changing trip.

After a long-awaited reunion with family and friends, Darwin chose to make his home in London. It was there that he wrote *The Voyage of the* Beagle, recounting the events of the global expedition. He contacted the scientists to whom he had sent specimens. He discussed their findings with them and continued to think about what he himself had seen. During this time, he became well known for his work on barnacles, coral reefs, and worms, and received awards for his contributions to science. He eventually became a member of the Royal Society of London for the Improvement of Natural Knowledge, the premier organization for scientists in England.

In London, however, Darwin began to show signs of severe illness. The heart palpitations, stomach problems, and other ailments he suffered suggest that he may have contracted a disease during the expedition. After marrying his cousin Emma Wedgwood (a practice that was both socially and legally acceptable in Victorian England), Darwin moved to a country estate with his new wife. The estate was called Down House and was far enough from London for Darwin to enjoy a healthier, easier lifestyle, yet close enough for him to maintain ties to his fellow scientists in the city.

DEVELOPMENT OF DARWIN'S THEORY

One of Darwin's colleagues, John Gould, was a leading expert on birds. After studying the specimens Darwin sent him, Gould concluded that the birds from the Galápagos were neither wrens nor mockingbirds. Instead, each was a different species of finch. There were 14 species total, all previously unknown. Each species was very similar to the others with the exception of their beaks.

Gould confirmed Darwin's belief that these Galápagos finches were similar to finches that live on the South American mainland. Darwin concluded that the islands must have been originally colonized by members of a single finch species from the South American mainland. At each island, the finches found a different set of organisms on which to feed. As the finches mated within their groups, their descendants became different, developing unique characteristics suited to their environments. Differences in the birds' beaks, for example, allowed them to eat different foods. Eventually, the differences became so pronounced that the birds could no longer reproduce with finches that had different features. Thus, they became different species.

The evidence of the finches, combined with other observations from the Galápagos, confirmed that species could change over time, a process Darwin originally called **transmutation**. He saw transmutation as a natural process whereby species change slowly in response to the demands of their environment. These ideas contradicted the widely held belief that all species were created in their present, unchanging form by supernatural forces. He shared his revolutionary ideas with only a few of his closest colleagues.

Darwin may have been reluctant to publish his ideas because of the recent publication of a book called *Vestiges of the Natural History of Creation*. This was one of the first books to openly address the ideas of the evolutionary change and origins of species. Although the book was published anonymously, many speculated that the Scottish geologist Robert Chambers was the author (a fact that was confirmed only after his death). There was a tremendous outcry against the book by scientists and the general public alike. While Darwin was a deeply religious man, he agreed with the idea that species could change. He found the scientific arguments in *Vestiges* weak, however, and realized that any theory that proposed the evolutionary change of species must have solid science behind its extraordinary claims if it was to be accepted by the scientific community.

Darwin had the evidence he needed, but he did not wish to publish his findings until he understood the mechanism that caused species to change. In 1838, however, he read a book titled *An Essay on the Principle of Population* written in 1798 by the English economist Thomas Robert Malthus. In this book, Malthus wrote that **populations** often grow to a size that exceeds the amount of available resources. When this happens, individuals must compete for resources. Individuals that can acquire resources will live and reproduce. Those that are unable to do so will not survive.

This "struggle for existence," as Darwin called it, was a critical realization for him. It provided him with a natural mechanism for change that allowed organisms to be better suited to their environment. He reasoned that individuals with traits that helped them survive in their environment would live to pass on those traits to their descendants. Those with traits ill-suited to their particular environment would not. Darwin named this process of passing on favorable traits and eliminating less favorable traits "natural selection."

Darwin realized that over long periods of time, natural selection could cause gradual changes in characteristics, what he called **descent with modification**. Fossils, livestock, crop species, and organisms living on islands gave Darwin clear evidence that natural selection could cause characteristics of a lineage (related individuals) to change over long periods of time so that later generations are very different from their distant ancestors. These changes will cause individuals to become better suited to the particular conditions where they live. Darwin also concluded that if individuals of one species are separated from one another under different environmental conditions, then natural selection can cause their offspring to develop differences that can lead to the formation of a new species. Natural selection causes the lineage of a new species to branch off from the original species, a process called **speciation**.

DARWIN AND WALLACE

Darwin spent over 20 years quietly developing his ideas on natural selection and descent with modification. He thought about his theory as he daily walked the path around his garden. Then, in 1858, he received a letter from a young naturalist named Alfred Russel Wallace who was working in the Malay Archipelago between southeastern Asia and Australia. Wallace sent Darwin a manuscript in

Figure 2.5 British naturalist Alfred Russel Wallace was a European naturalist who worked in South America and the South Pacific.

Alfred Russel Wallace

Despite having his theory of natural selection and evolution overshadowed by Darwin's, Wallace did become famous for other scientific contributions. He worked extensively in the field of **biogeography**, writing about the way different kinds of plants and animals are distributed around the Earth. From his extensive work in the islands of the Malay Archipelago between the South Pacific and Indian oceans, Wallace noticed that animals in the western islands of Borneo and Sumatra are similar to animals from Asia, while animals in the more eastern islands of Sulawesi are similar to animals from Australia. The boundary separating the Asian and Australian zones of species has been named the **Wallace Line** in his honor. Wallace was also one of the first scientists to think about the future of the environment. He wrote numerous papers about the effects of deforestation, as well as other ways that humans adversely affect the environment.

which he described how species change over time. He wanted Darwin to read the manuscript and help him publish it. Darwin was immediately struck by the incredible similarity between his ideas and those of Wallace.

The men made similar observations independently of one another. Both saw that (1) there are differences in traits among individuals in a population, such that within that population, some individuals have traits that help them survive better than other individuals; (2) populations that are isolated from one another can become very different from one another; and (3) many organisms have structures that are modified for different purposes but are composed of the same fundamental parts, a phenomenon known as **homology**.

Darwin shared Wallace's letter and manuscript with several colleagues, who decided to present both men's work to the leading scientists in London, a premier group known as the Linnaean Society.

The Linnaean Society, named after Carl Linnaeus, was established in 1788. It remains to this day a preeminent forum for discussion of natural history, **genetics**, and other biological topics.

On July 1, 1858, Darwin's and Wallace's papers were presented to the Linnaean Society by Sir Charles Lyell (the geologist whose work Darwin had read while aboard the *Beagle*) and the equally well-known and respected botanist Dr. J.D. Hooker. That day was one of the great moments in science. Many of those in attendance were amazed by the elegance, simplicity, and strength of the process Darwin and Wallace described. Upon hearing Darwin's description of natural selection, Darwin's close friend and colleague Thomas Huxley is reported to have said in reference to himself, "How extremely stupid not to have thought of that!"

ON THE ORIGIN OF SPECIES BY NATURAL SELECTION

Although similar to Wallace's, Darwin's arguments for natural selection were better developed and thus more readily accepted by the scientific community. With this support, Darwin worked to finish the manuscript that would eventually become his famous book titled *On the Origin of Species by Natural Selection*, or, as it is more commonly called, *The Origin of Species*. When it was published on November 24, 1859, it sold out immediately.

As with Chambers's *Vestiges of the Natural History of Creation*, many people considered Darwin's work heresy. Individuals in the scientific, political, and religious communities vehemently attacked Darwin and his work. Most scientists, however, accepted Darwin's conclusions and began to use his ideas as a new direction for their own scientific studies. With the publication of *The Origin of Species* and the fundamental natural processes he described, Darwin had changed the very nature of biology.

Darwin chose not to engage in the public controversy surrounding his book. Some of his colleagues, however, did not shy away from the firestorm Darwin had sparked. Huxley engaged in numerous public debates with antievolutionists such as Archbishop Samuel

Wilberforce and famed **paleontologist** Richard Owen. Huxley's tenacious support of natural selection and evolution earned him the nickname "Darwin's Bulldog."

While the debate over evolution and natural selection raged, Darwin continued to write. In *The Descent of Man*, Darwin described his ideas on human evolution. Another groundbreaking book, *On the Different Forms of Flowers on Plants of the Same Species*, described the evolution of flowers. It became one of the most important books on plant reproduction. Although his other writings contained evolutionary ideas and themes, no other book was attacked as ferociously as *The Origin of Species*.

After a long and productive life, Charles Darwin died at his home on April 19, 1882. By parliamentary consent, he was interred at Westminster Abbey. His pallbearers included such prominent figures as the Duke of Argyll, the Duke of Devonshire, James Lowell (the American ambassador to Britain), J.D. Hooker, Thomas Huxley, Alfred Russel Wallace, and William Spottiswoode (president of the Royal Society of London). Fittingly, Darwin was laid to rest near the tomb of another English scientist who changed the world: the physicist Sir Isaac Newton.

SUMMARY

Charles Darwin was an English naturalist who used keen observation skills and clear scientific thought to develop the scientific theory of evolution by natural selection. Darwin's interest in science began at a young age and led him eventually to travel around the Earth on the HMS *Beagle*. Although he noted many interesting phenomena throughout the voyage, it was his observations of plants and animals on the Galápagos Islands that provided critical evidence for the power of natural selection. Although Darwin's ideas are still debated, he is widely regarded as one of the greatest contributors to the field of biology.

Mendel and Inheritance

From this strong principle of inheritance, any selected variety
will tend to propagate its new and modified form.
—*Charles Darwin,* The Origin of Species

Farmers have always worked to find new traits for the plants and animals they raise. Whether it is a cow that produces more milk or a potato that is more resistant to disease, breeders are always looking for individuals with pleasing traits that can be spread to later generations. This desire for improvement led to the development of wheat, corn, rice, apples, grapes, and a number of other important crops. For thousands of years, humans slowly and successfully changed their crops and livestock, causing desirable traits to be passed from parents to offspring, without understanding exactly how it happened.

Darwin and his contemporaries held a general belief that particles in the male and female known as **gemmules** contained the information needed to make a particular structure. It was thought that during mating, these gemmules migrated from every part of the body and simply combined to form the offspring. This simple and attractive hypothesis seemed to explain quite neatly why a red-flowered plant mated with a white-flowered plant produces pink flowers.

Unfortunately, it does not explain why, in some species, this mating produces not pink, but either red or white flowers. Nor does it explain why color that is absent in one generation may unexpectedly reappear in a later generation. The process of how traits are passed from parent to offspring would remain a scientific mystery until a young monk named Gregor Mendel solved the problem by growing peas in his monastery garden.

GREGOR MENDEL AND THE PEAS

Christened Johann in 1822, Mendel changed his first name to Gregor 21 years later when he joined the Augustinian monastery at Brno (now in the Czech Republic). It was there that he combined his extensive knowledge of mathematics and botany in a series of experiments that would lay the foundation for modern genetics.

Mendel knew from the work of other scientists that certain plants could be bred to produce a trait consistently from parent to offspring, a condition known as **true-breeding**. The common garden pea (*Pisum sativum*) was one such plant, with true-breeding **varieties** having traits such as white or purple flowers, green or yellow seeds, and wrinkled or smooth seeds. Because of this, Mendel used the pea for his experiments, choosing parental plants that were true-breeding for certain traits.

In his breeding experiments with flower color, Mendel removed the male parts from true-breeding purple flowered plants so they could not self-fertilize. Then he crossed that plant with a true-breeding white flowered plant by transferring **pollen** (containing the male gamete, or sperm) from the white flowers to the **stigma** (a female reproductive structure where the pollen germinates and guides the sperm to the female gamete, or egg) of the purple flowers. The seeds from this mating were planted and allowed to flower. All offspring from this first generation (F_1 **generation**) had purple flowers like their female parent.

Next, Mendel crossed two of the purple-flowered F_1 plants. Offspring resulting from this mating (F_2 **generation**) produced mostly purple-flowered plants, but also some white-flowered plants. Though other scientists had produced similar results, Mendel was the first to count the number of plants with purple versus white flowers and record the ratio. He observed that approximately

75% of the F_2 generation had purple flowers and 25% had white flowers: a 3:1 ratio. Mendel repeated the experiment with other true-breeding traits and found that one trait consistently disappeared

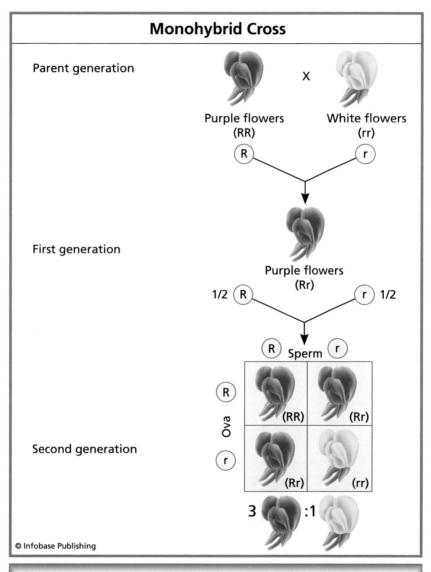

Figure 3.1   In one of Mendel's experiments, he cross-pollinated two true-breeding flowers, one purple and one white. The first generation's offspring all displayed purple petals, but the second generation produced some purple flowers, and some white. This led Mendel to conclude that some traits, like the purple flower, are dominant, and some, like the white flower, are recessive.

Basic Genetic Terms

When Mendel conducted his studies, he had to describe principles and ideas without the help of an established scientific vocabulary. Scientists have since identified and developed terms for the phenomena Mendel discovered and described. Scientists now know that the inherited material containing the information of life is **deoxyribonucleic acid (DNA)**. DNA is organized into chromosomes, structures made of DNA. Typically, an individual receives one set of chromosomes from the mother's egg and another set of chromosomes from the father's sperm, so that each cell contains two complete sets of chromosomes. The basic functional units on these chromosomes that control traits are known as genes. Different forms of a gene are called alleles, which can be symbolized using letters such as *A* and *a* to identify different alleles. The combination of alleles within an individual is the genotype. If the two alleles in an individual are the same (i.e., *AA* or *aa*), the genotype is called **homozygous**. If the two alleles are different (i.e., *Aa*), the genotype is called **heterozygous**. The offspring of two parents of different breeds or varieties of plant is called a **hybrid**.

in the F_1 generation only to reappear in approximately 25% of F_2 individuals.

MENDEL'S LAW OF SEGREGATION

Based upon these experiments, Mendel concluded that each individual received two particles, one from the mother's egg and one from the father's sperm. The two particles combined during mating to produce features, such as flower color, observed in the offspring. These observable features are known as an organism's **phenotype**.

Mendel was fortunate to have chosen plant characteristics in which one trait is **dominant** to the other **recessive** trait. The dominant trait is expressed in all the F_1 offspring. For example, purple flower color is dominant to white, round seeds are dominant to wrinkled, and yellow seeds are dominant to green. Mendel used letters such as *P* for the dominant purple **allele** and *p* for the recessive white allele, two forms of the **gene** controlling flower color. The **genotype** of a true-breeding plant with purple flowers would be symbolized by *PP* because it came from parents who contributed a *P* allele from the egg and a *P* allele from the sperm. Similarly, a true-breeding white-flowered plant would be symbolized by *pp* because each parent contributed a *p* allele. When homozygous dominant

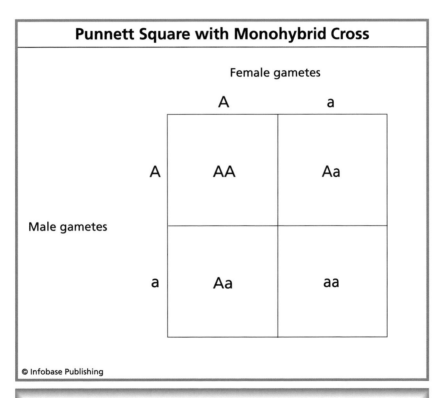

Figure 3.2 The Punnett square is a useful tool for determining possible trait expression in offspring. The alleles shown in the boxes of the square are possible offspring that could result from a pairing of two parent organisms, which are shown above and to the left in the diagram.

purple-flowered plants (*PP*) are crossed with homozygous recessive white-flowered plants (*pp*), all the offspring are heterozygous (*Pp*) with the purple flower phenotype because they receive a dominant *P* allele from one parent and a recessive *p* allele from the other.

Mendel observed that when heterozygous *Pp* plants are crossed with one another, the *P* and *p* combine in three different ways: *PP*, *Pp*, and *pp*, always in a 3:1 ratio when the purple and white phenotypes are counted. From these results, Mendel developed his first law of heredity, also called the **law of segregation**. It states that the paired alleles separate during gamete formation in the parents and are joined together in the offspring.

Other Dominance Relationships

Mendel worked with traits that had a specific dominant-recessive relationship. Other traits, however, have different dominance relationships. In plants such as snapdragons and carnations, the homozygous dominant genotype produces red flowers, the homozygous recessive genotype produces white flowers, and the heterozygous genotype produces pink flowers. This is called **incomplete dominance**.

Codominance occurs when neither allele is fully dominant. The human ABO blood groups are a perfect example of codominance. For human blood groups, there are three alleles: I^A, I^B, and i. $I^A I^A$ and $I^A i$ genotypes produce type A blood. $I^B I^B$ and $I^B i$ genotypes produce type B blood. $I^A I^B$ heterozygotes have the AB blood type, and ii genotypes have type O blood. Because of their blood cells' unique features, individuals with type A blood cannot receive transfusions of type B blood, and vice versa. Individuals with type O blood can receive only type O blood, but can donate blood to individuals with any blood type (a person with type O blood is known as a *universal donor*). Individuals with AB blood can receive any type of blood (*universal recipient*), but donate only to type AB individuals.

MENDEL'S LAW OF INDEPENDENT ASSORTMENT

Mendel repeated his experiments using plants that were true-breeding for two traits. As before, traits disappeared in the F_1 and reappeared in the F_2. For example, plants having round, yellow peas crossed with plants having wrinkled, green peas produced F_1 offspring having round, yellow peas. When these F_1 offspring were crossed, however, they produced four different types of peas: round/yellow, round/green, wrinkled/yellow, and wrinkled/green in a 9:3:3:1 ratio, respectively.

While the basic aspects of segregation still applied to these crosses, two sets of traits were now segregating. For example, plants with the dominant traits of round, yellow seeds (*RRYY*) produced only *RY* gametes, and plants with the recessive wrinkled, green seeds (*rryy*) produced only *ry* gametes. Offspring from these crosses were all *RrYy*. Unlike their parents, however, these plants could produce four different types of gametes: *RY*, *Ry*, *rY*, and *ry*. When these are combined, they produce four different phenotypes in a 9:3:3:1 ratio.

Mendel's second law of inheritance, also known as the **law of independent assortment**, explains this phenomenon by stating that different traits segregate independently of one another. In other words, green seeds are not always wrinkled and yellow seeds are not always round.

It is important to note, however, that Mendel's second law holds true only for traits that are controlled by genes found on different **chromosomes**. Traits controlled by genes on the same chromosome, known as **linked traits**, will not segregate independently of one another and will display other patterns of inheritance.

THE MODERN SYNTHESIS

Mendel published the results of his research in 1865 in a paper titled "Experiments on Plant Hybridization," which described his **theory of particulate inheritance**. With his thoughtful experimental design and careful collection and analysis of data, he made

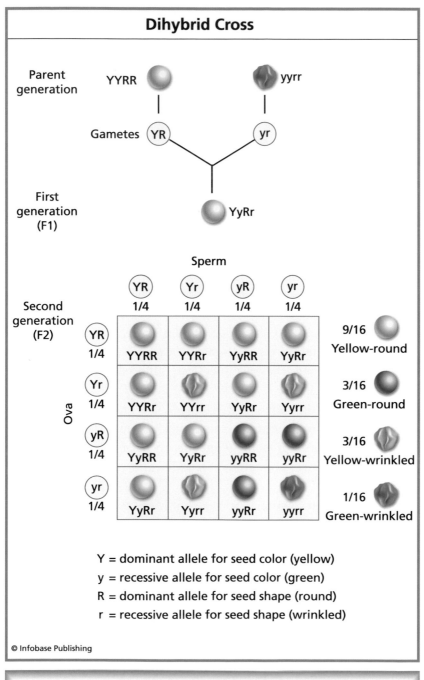

Dihybrid Cross

Parent generation — YYRR ⚪ 🟤 yyrr

Gametes (YR) (yr)

First generation (F1) — ⚪ YyRr

Sperm

	YR 1/4	Yr 1/4	yR 1/4	yr 1/4	
YR 1/4	YYRR	YYRr	YyRR	YyRr	9/16 Yellow-round
Yr 1/4	YYRr	YYrr	YyRr	Yyrr	3/16 Green-round
yR 1/4	YyRR	YyRr	yyRR	yyRr	3/16 Yellow-wrinkled
yr 1/4	YyRr	Yyrr	yyRr	yyrr	1/16 Green-wrinkled

Second generation (F2) — Ova

Y = dominant allele for seed color (yellow)
y = recessive allele for seed color (green)
R = dominant allele for seed shape (round)
r = recessive allele for seed shape (wrinkled)

© Infobase Publishing

Figure 3.3 In one experiment, Mendel tested the inheritance of two separate traits in pea plants—color and texture of skin. The first generation produced offspring with the dominant traits of yellow color and smooth skin. The second-generation offspring included an assortment of expressions of both traits.

one of the greatest discoveries in the history of science. Today, he is widely regarded as the "Father of Genetics." Despite unlocking one of the greatest scientific mysteries of all time, Mendel's work was not immediately appreciated. In fact, his findings were largely ignored for many years, because biologists did not realize their significance and relevance to biology. One scientific urban legend states that Darwin actually had a copy of Mendel's groundbreaking research but that he never read it. Had Darwin read Mendel's paper, some speculate that this would have provided him with the genetic component he needed to further strengthen his already powerful argument. Other science historians, however, claim that even if Darwin had read Mendel's paper, it is unlikely he would have understood how the mathematical arguments Mendel presented to explain inheritance would have related to his description of natural selection.

Non-Mendelian Traits

Mendel was extremely fortunate in the traits he chose to study because the genes controlling the traits behaved in a way that made it possible for him to understand the fundamental features of inheritance. This is now called **Mendelian inheritance**. There are some traits, however, that have **non-Mendelian inheritance**. Conditions such as color blindness, some forms of baldness, and hemophilia are recessive traits controlled by genes on the X chromosome. These conditions are much more common in males than females, because males have an X chromosome and a Y chromosome (XY genotype). Therefore any trait (dominant or recessive) found on the X chromosome will automatically be expressed. Females have two X chromosomes (XX genotype), and therefore a recessive allele on one X chromosome can be masked by a dominant allele on the other X chromosome. Non-Mendelian traits do not occur in F_1 and F_2 generations with the same frequencies expected for Mendelian traits, but rather follow their own predictable frequencies of occurrence.

In the early 1900s, however, scientists rediscovered Mendel's work and made the connection with Darwin's process of natural selection. These biologists realized that changes in DNA called **mutations** were responsible for making new and different alleles of genes and, consequently, new phenotypes. As scientists considered the conceptual links between Darwin's and Mendel's discoveries, they realized that mutation, natural selection, and inheritance work together to produce evolutionary change. They now understood that the phenotypic variation Darwin wrote about in regards to populations was caused by different alleles that are inherited according to processes Mendel described. The different alleles are produced by mutation. While most mutations are harmful, some are beneficial and spread throughout a population by natural selection.

The combination of Darwinian and Mendelian principles has been called the **modern synthesis**. The researchers who combined these ideas developed testable models using mathematical methods to describe precisely how natural selection can cause predictable changes over time in the frequencies of alleles, genotypes, and phenotypes. For example, the researchers Godfrey Hardy (1877–1947) and Wilhelm Weinberg (1862–1937) discovered independently of one another that if one knows the frequencies of alleles in populations, one can predict the frequencies of different genotypes found in the population. If genotypes are not within the predicted frequency, a scientist can then investigate whether natural selection or other evolutionary forces are acting on a population. Their discovery, known as the **Hardy-Weinberg principle**, has become a fundamental concept in evolutionary biology.

The contributions of many scientists led to the development of the modern definition of *evolution* as "changes in allele frequencies within a population over time." In addition to increasing the scientific understanding of natural selection, these researchers identified other processes such as **genetic drift**, in which small population size causes random changes in allele frequencies within populations without the action of natural selection. The efforts of biologists working during the period of the modern synthesis confirmed, however, that natural selection is the only evolutionary mechanism that can lead to evolution and the refinement of adaptations. Therefore, the addition of Mendel's principles to Darwin's theory completed the understanding of how the process of inheritance explains how both artificial and natural selection work. It provided the missing piece of the puzzle, mutation, which provides the raw material of genetic variation that natural selection can act upon to produce change. These studies led one of the main scientists behind modern synthesis, Theodosius Dobzhansky (1900–1975), to remark, "Nothing in biology makes sense except in the light of evolution."

SUMMARY

Although humans had known for thousands of years that traits are passed from parents to offspring, it was not until the work of Gregor Mendel that this process was understood. Through his experiments breeding pea plants, Mendel determined that individuals contain pairs of alleles. One member of the pair is inherited from the mother, and the other is inherited from the father. The alleles combine in offspring and, depending on the dominance relationship between the alleles, cause predictable traits in the offspring. Mendel also determined that in some instances alleles for different traits are shuffled and passed to offspring independently of one another. Although the importance of his work was not immediately recognized, scientists later determined its significance not only in providing the foundation principles of genetics, but also as a mechanism for Darwin's process of natural selection.

Artificial Selection

*Not one of our domestic animals can be named
which has not in some country drooping ears.*
—*Charles Darwin,* The Origin of Species

In 2006, a young thoroughbred horse named Barbaro captured the attention of the horseracing world with a commanding win at the Kentucky Derby. Barbaro's strength, speed, and love of racing were the stuff of legends. His pedigree could be traced to one of three stallions brought to England at the end of the seventeenth century. His ancestor the Godolphin Arabian and the other two stallions, the Darley Arabian and the Byerly Turk, were bred with English mares in the hopes of producing faster, stronger horses. All modern thoroughbreds are descended from these three stallions.

For hundreds of years, winning owners have tried to build on their successes by breeding desired traits into future generations. These carefully planned and documented matings have resulted in animals of unbelievable speed and stamina. Unfortunately for the fleet-footed Barbaro, however, an impressive pedigree could not prevent disaster. Two weeks after his win in Kentucky, he fractured three bones in one of his back legs during his run at the Preakness Stakes. He was euthanized eight months later because of complications from the injury.

Such incidents are not uncommon in racehorses. One possible explanation for this may be that the skeletons of today's thorough-bred horses are incapable of supporting the larger musculature imposed on them by generations of **selective breeding**. If this is true, owners may have to consider the need for stronger, heavier bones in their run for the roses.

ARTIFICIAL SELECTION

Artificial selection, the process of choosing and mating only those plants and animals that have desired traits, provides numerous examples of how an individual's ability to breed or survive better than others can lead to changes in the species. It was from observing examples of artificial selection that Darwin developed the basic principles of natural selection. Darwin was familiar with the process of selective breeding in plants and animals. He referred to this human-guided process as artificial selection and used it as strong evidence to support his argument for natural selection. The only difference between the two processes is that in artificial selection, humans decide which individuals pass their traits on to offspring, while in natural selection, the environment influences which individuals survive and reproduce.

Darwin was quite familiar with the concept of selective breeding. From his experience with livestock and his participation in the gentlemanly hobby of pigeon breeding, he knew that over generations a breeder could eventually change the appearance of an animal or plant. For example, the common rock pigeon (*Columba livia*) is a relatively plain-looking bird. Native to southern Europe and northern Africa, it is now common (and frequently undesired) in parks and cities throughout the world. Humans first began keeping pigeons several thousand years ago. Breeders chose male and female birds with interesting variations of feathers, colors, neck, beak shape, or flying behaviors and allowed them to breed. Over several generations, these traits became more pronounced in their offspring until the features were well established in the birds. Thus, we now have different varieties, or **breeds,** of pigeons, such as the fan tail, archangel, and tumbler, each with its own distinct features.

Figure 4.1   These four different breeds of pigeon illustrate the results of artificial selection.

A variety or breed refers to a specific type of an animal or plant species that has been selectively bred to have characteristic traits that they pass on to their offspring. Varieties and breeds are still members of the same species, but have traits that distinguish them from other members of the species. Thus, there are now breeds of pigeon that are very different in appearance from each other as well as their common ancestor, the rock pigeon. As long as organisms mate only within their breed, the differences will be maintained. If different breeds mate, however, the differences will not be as pronounced.

Darwin reasoned that if breeders were capable of producing these distinct differences through artificial selection, then the environment could drive the same changes in nature, whereby traits that promoted survival would also become more common over time. The only difference is that through natural selection the extent of changes eventually could lead to the formation of new, different species.

Examples of Artificial Selection

Artificial selection has occurred since humans first **domesticated** various animal and plant species. Indeed, the rise of human culture has been strongly tied to this activity. One need only look at different breeds of dogs, cats, sheep, fruits, and vegetables to see the results of artificial selection. One example that provides a particularly interesting example of artificial selection in action is cattle.

Cattle (*Bos taurusi*) were first domesticated by humans between 7,500 and 10,000 years ago from a now extinct species called an auroch (*Bos primigenius*). Individual cattle were originally chosen for breeding based upon their ability to supply milk or meat and their ability to serve as draft animals on farms. Because of their dual use for food and labor, early cattle tended to be fairly large animals with lower quality meat. Typically, cattle were eaten only when they were no longer useful for draft purposes.

When horses replaced cattle as laboring draft animals, some breeders began to focus on improving the quality of their cattle's meat. Breeders in Britain in particular began to focus on developing cattle that were smaller and produced more meat at a younger age. One such breed is the Hereford, which was originally developed by Benjamin Tomkins, a farmer in Herefordshire, England. He and other farmers in the area had been working to develop a breed of cattle that could rapidly produce high-quality meat by grazing on their local grasses. After numerous attempts, Tomkins successfully bred a young bull with two cows named Pidgeon and Mottle in 1742. This mating produced a hardy breed of cattle that could graze on native grasses and produce meat quickly, maturing in two years as opposed to the typical four to five. With these highly desirable traits, Herefords quickly spread throughout British farms.

Herefords were eventually brought to the United States in the early 1800s, and by 1840 several breeding herds had been established. As the breed became more popular, ranchers formed the American Hereford Association to keep track of the different Hereford bloodlines. One particularly important bull named Anxiety 4

Figure 4.2 The auroch (*top*) is the ancestor of today's domestic cattle (*bottom*). The auroch became extinct in the seventeenth century.

became known as the "Father of American Herefords" because he was bred so extensively that nearly all American Hereford cattle can trace their ancestry back to him.

In the 1930s, Hereford breeders began to select for smaller, rapidly maturing cattle that fattened at an early age, so-called baby beef. Dwarfism became common in the breed at this time. In the 1950s, however, consumers no longer wanted fatty cuts of beef, so ranchers began to choose cattle with larger frames that produced more meat with less fat, thereby changing the features of the breed once again.

The Hereford also gave rise to another popular breed, the Polled, or hornless, Hereford. Horns often need to be removed from cattle so they cannot hurt themselves, other cattle, or people. A naturally hornless, or **polled**, calf is highly desirable. In 1891, a Hereford breeder from Iowa named Warren Gammons took advantage of calves with this unusual trait and started the first breeding herd of Polled Herefords, which became a popular breed. Polled Herefords are not the only hornless breed of cattle. The Angus breed, which originated in Scotland, has always been polled. There are even historical records of polled cattle breeds in Siberia and ancient Egypt.

Dairy farmers have made the same strides toward improved milk production as ranchers have moved toward improved meat production. The Guernsey was bred to produce milk with a high butterfat content while consuming less feed than other dairy cattle. The easily recognized Holsteins, with their characteristic black-and-white coloration, were bred for their high level of milk production. The Jersey breed was selected and bred not only for its milk production, but also for its ability to tolerate heat better than other breeds of dairy cattle. Clearly, the various needs and desires of the farmer and the consumer have led to the development of many special breeds whose features meet those needs.

Animals are not the only organisms to have experienced artificial selection. Plants have also been the focus of breeders' and farmers' attention. Many of our cereal crops have been subjected to artificial selection for thousands of years. Wheat (*Triticum aestivum*), a grass, was one of the first crops domesticated by humans. Researchers believe that an ancestor of modern wheat called emmer wheat (*Triticum turgidum*) was first eaten as food by humans more than 19,000 years ago. Eventually, people began to collect and plant seeds to grow their own foods, and by 10,000 years ago, humans had domesticated wheat. Since that time, farmers have selected for specific traits. One of the first desirable traits was the production of "nonshattering" seeds. In most grasses, the seeds fall off the plant when they mature, but in nonshattering plants, the seeds remain attached to the plant at maturity. This trait allows for a much easier harvest, because seeds may be plucked en masse directly from the plant rather than having to be picked up one at a time from the ground. Seeds that were saved from the nonshattering plants were planted the following years, allowing the trait to become more common in early wheat. Archaeologists have also noticed that over time, the seeds of wheat plants became larger and more numerous. Both of

Radiation to Variation

Crop breeders depend on new traits to arise in individuals that they can then exploit in a breeding program. They are limited, however, by the rate at which natural, spontaneous mutations occur in the DNA and by the ability to identify those mutations in individuals. Some researchers speed up the process. Instead of waiting for nature to make a new mutation in the DNA, they expose seeds to radiation, mutating the DNA with gamma rays. Seedlings grown from these treated seeds are then screened for desired traits. Through this method, scientists have produced varieties of cocoa (*Theobroma cacao*), rice (*Oryza sativa*), pears (*Pyrus* spp.), barley (*Hordeum vulgare*), sunflowers (*Helianthus annuus*), cotton (*Gossypium* spp.), peppermint (*Mentha piperita*), and a number of other plants that have greater disease resistance, increased yield, better taste, larger size, or broader tolerance for climate and other environmental conditions. The new plants are safe, as the radiation eventually wears off and is not passed on to their offspring. Although the radiation increases the occurrence of new mutations, the researchers cannot direct or control what trait will mutate. This same uncontrollability exists in nature, where mutations occur in the DNA is still random—"a roll of the dice," as one researcher describes it. The researchers are simply helping the process along.

these are important traits that would have allowed breeders to improve their crop yields.

Corn (*Zea maize*) is another important crop that has undergone extensive artificial selection. Early farmers grew an ancestor of modern corn called **teosinte** that was quite unlike our modern crop. This plant had small, hard kernels that grew on multiple small branches. Farmers chose and selectively bred plants that had larger, softer kernels. Eventually, the traits of the plant changed to such an extent that it became the corn we now enjoy. Researchers have even identified some of the specific genes that our agricultural ancestors unknowingly changed through their selective breeding.

SELECTION CAN BRING MAJOR CHANGES

An important aspect of selection that must be remembered is that it does not act on single genes alone. Genes are organized on chromosomes, and a single chromosome contains genes for many different traits. This can best be illustrated by an experiment conducted on the Russian silver fox (*Vulpes vulpes*), an animal that is wary of humans and quite aggressive in the wild. Researchers interested in the domestication of dogs wondered what changes would occur if they conducted artificial selection on a wild canine species.

The researchers established a simple criterion: to selectively choose and breed the most docile individuals. In as few as eight generations, the researchers noted major changes in the animals. Instead of the uniform coat color typical of Russian silver foxes, the animals developed new coloration patterns, such as large patches and star-shaped whitening in the face. Drooping ears replaced erect ones. Tails were held higher and curled over the back in contrast to the low, straight tails of the wild animals. Eventually, later generations even began to lick the humans' hands and whimper. This experiment clearly demonstrates that selection acting on one trait, tameness, is tied to changes in a number of other traits that were not selected by the researchers.

Breeding Man's Best Friend

It is not difficult to imagine making small changes among different breeds of cattle or horses. The outcome of artificial selection, however, becomes more difficult to consider when one thinks about the tremendous differences in size, shape, and other features among different breeds of dogs. How can anything, even something as powerful as artificial selection, produce breeds as dramatically different in size and shape as border collies, Chihuahuas, English bulldogs, Irish wolfhounds, and Siberian huskies? Developmental biologists have discovered that the variation in appearance among these breeds is due in part to differences in rates of development of the skull, legs, jaws, and other features that cause the different sizes and shapes that characterize these breeds. For example, the snout and jaw develops a longer shape in border collies than bulldogs, in which jaw development is truncated. Irish wolfhounds, one of the largest breeds, have a much longer period of growth and development than that of the Chihuahua, one of the smallest breeds. Mating individuals within the same breed (artificial selection) perpetuates these traits, sometimes to the detriment of the animal. Some breeds, for example, tend to live much shorter lives because of health problems associated with tremendous size (in the case of the wolfhound) and short snout (in the case of the bulldog).

GENETIC VARIATION IS ESSENTIAL FOR SELECTION

The question that must be addressed in both artificial and natural selection is: Where do these acted upon traits come from? The answer is mutation. Changes in the genetic material (DNA) produce new characteristics. Most DNA mutations are harmful, such as when a mutation leads to a genetic disease. Some, however, are clearly not.

In all of the preceding examples, breeders intentionally bred individuals that had novel, desirable traits, thereby producing successive generations with enhanced versions of the traits.

The ability for traits to be passed from parents to offspring, and the extent to which a trait is controlled by genes, refers to traits' **heritability**. All traits in an individual are controlled by both genetics and the environment. The size of a plant, for example, will be controlled by genes for height as well as the environmental conditions in which the plant grows (i.e., water, sunlight, and soil nutrients). A plant growing in nutrient-poor soil will be smaller than one that receives large quantities of fertilizer. This is an example of an environmental effect. If several plants of the same species are grown in the same soil, however, some will be taller than others. This is an example of a genetic effect. Natural and artificial selection can only act on heritable traits that can be passed on to their offspring. This is the reason why Lamarck's theory was not correct—acquired traits caused by the environment are not heritable and cannot be passed on to later generations. Genetic-based traits, however, such as those chosen by the cattle, wheat, corn, and fox breeders, are heritable. Therefore, natural and artificial selection depend on heritable genetic variation in order for either type of selection to produce change over time.

SUMMARY

Artificial selection is a process in which humans choose and selectively breed different individuals of domesticated plants or animals to spread or enhance traits. The process simply involves finding males and females with the desired traits, and then allowing them to breed over many generations. This process has produced dramatic changes in a number of different crops and domesticated animals for a variety of different traits. The critical aspect of artificial selection is that the trait must be under genetic control and there must be genetic variation for the trait that the breeder can then select. Artificial selection provided a powerful example that helped illustrate Darwin's ideas about natural selection.

Natural Selection

*I have called this principle, by which each slight variation,
if useful, is preserved, by the term Natural Selection.*
—Charles Darwin, The Origin of Species

The peppered moth (*Biston betularia*) is common in Britain. It gets its name from its peppered appearance; most individuals are whitish with black speckles on their wings. In 1848, naturalists were surprised to discover a completely black form of the moth. Within 40 years, these dark moths outnumbered their speckled brethren in certain locations, sometimes by as much as 90%.

The mystery of the peppered moth's dramatic change was solved by a British ecologist named H.B.D. Kettlewell in 1955. He noticed that with the coming of the industrial revolution, soot from English factories accumulated on tree trunks, making their bark much darker than usual. Kettlewell predicted that the change in the color of the bark was related to the change in the color of the moths. To test his hypothesis, he placed both types of moths on both types of trees. He found that birds ate more black moths on soot-free, light-colored bark and more speckled moths on sooty bark. Kettlewell concluded that the increase in the frequency of black moths was caused by the effects of pollution on the trees, a phenomenon known as **industrial melanism**.

Figure 5.1 The black moth and the speckled moth seen here are different forms of the same species, called the peppered moth. As seen here, the speckled moth is better camouflaged in areas where there is lots of lichen growth on trees. The black moth would be better camouflaged in polluted areas where the tree trunks are darker.

Industrial melanism is a classic example of natural selection. In unpolluted forests, speckled moths are at an advantage because their lighter coloration camouflages them. Black moths, however, are more visible on the light trunks and consequently are eaten more frequently. The advantage is reversed in areas with industrial pollution that darkens tree trunks with soot; black moths are protected by their camouflage, while speckled individuals are more easily seen and eaten more often.

Despite minor problems in some of Kettlewell's experimental designs, scientists continue to support his fundamental conclusions. Modern researchers have modified Kettlewell's experiments and used new technology to study industrial melanism further. They have shown that coloration in peppered moths is a genetically controlled trait and that selection caused by birds and other predators can change the frequency of speckled and black moths as predicted by the theory of natural selection.

The idea behind natural selection is that some individuals will survive and/or reproduce better than others will. This measure of survival and reproductive success among individuals is called **fitness**. Darwin reasoned that if fitness traits can be passed from parent to offspring, they will become more common in a population over time, because individuals with higher fitness pass on these traits to a greater extent than individuals with lower fitness. This results in a population of individuals better suited to the conditions of their particular environment.

For example, imagine a type of plant that produces individuals with red, pink, or white flowers. Now suppose the local **pollinators** (animals that move pollen from one plant to another) prefer red flowers (perhaps the red flowers are easier to see or perhaps they produce tastier nectar). Pollination produces seeds. Seeds produce new plants. Therefore, if a pollinator visits more red flowers than pink or white and if flower color is a genetically controlled trait that passes from parent to offspring, then plants with red flowers will become more common in that particular area.

Scientists explain this phenomenon in genetic terms. Suppose this plant's flower color is controlled by one gene with two alleles. The dominant allele (R) causes red flower color, while the recessive allele (r) causes white flower color. Individuals with the RR genotype produce red flowers, those with the Rr genotype produce pink flowers, and those with the rr genotype produce white flowers. If plants with red flowers are pollinated more often, allowing them to produce more seeds, the R allele, and therefore red flower color, will become more common in the population.

Now, for the same species of plant, suppose that the pollinators in a different location prefer white flowers over pink or red. In this

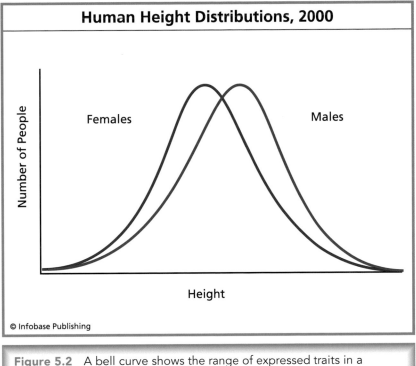

Figure 5.2   A bell curve shows the range of expressed traits in a population. The bell curve shown here indicates that there are fewer very short and very tall people (at either end of the bell shape) and a much larger number of people distributed in the middle range of height (the tall part of the bell shape).

different environment, white flowers will reproduce more. Therefore, the *r* allele and white flowers will become more common over time.

It is important to understand that natural selection "chooses" and acts upon the phenotype. This in turn causes population-wide changes in genotype and allele frequency. In the example above, pollinators are choosing the flower-color phenotype and consequently changing the allele frequencies over time. Such changes are the basis of evolution and adaptation.

Not all traits are controlled by a single gene with two alleles. Some traits are controlled by multiple alleles or multiple genes, or they may involve an interaction between genetic and environmental factors. In such situations, there will be a range of phenotypic traits expressed in a population. For example, human height is controlled by environmental effects as well as a number of genes, resulting in a continuous range of heights. A graph of the heights of many different individuals produces a bell-shaped curve, in which there are few extremely short or tall individuals, but many of intermediate height. This *bell curve* occurs for many biological characteristics. Natural selection acts on these traits in the same way that it acts on those with a limited number of clearly defined conditions.

THREE TYPES OF NATURAL SELECTION

Scientists have measured natural selection for a variety of traits in many species and have identified three general patterns of how selection can act on traits in a population: **directional selection**, **stabilizing selection**, and **disruptive selection**. To understand the differences among these types of selection, it is best to consider a trait that can have a range of conditions, such as dark to light or small to large.

Directional Selection

Directional selection occurs when one extreme phenotype is favored over the opposite extreme phenotype. Alleles producing the favored trait increase in the population, while alleles being selected against gradually decrease in frequency and may ultimately be eliminated from the population. In the case of the peppered moth, for example, the polluted forest environment caused intense directional selection by selecting for the dark-colored moths and selecting against the light-colored moths. The dark phenotype and the alleles causing it increased at the same time that the light phenotype and the alleles causing it decreased. In unpolluted forests, directional selection favors light moths, while dark moths are selected against.

Selection does not allow for limitless change. It must operate within the existing genetic variation. For example, selection can cause peppered moths to have black offspring, but it will not allow them to have purple offspring unless a new genetic mutation occurs.

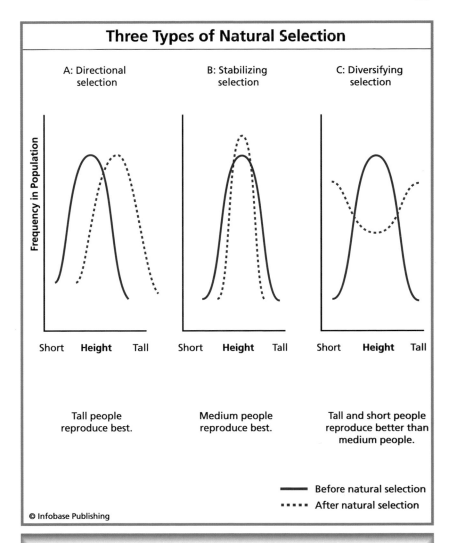

Figure 5.3 The bell curves shown here illustrate three different kinds of selection. The graphs at the top indicate the distribution of height in a human population. If tall people in this population reproduce more than short or medium-sized people, directional selection leads to an increase in height of the overall population. If medium people reproduce more, stabilizing selection maintains the average height of the population without much change. If medium-sized people reproduce the least, diversifying selection leads to there being more short and tall people, with few medium-sized people.

Another example of directional selection is the evolution of **antibiotic resistance** in bacteria. Widespread and often inappropriate use of antibiotics has caused strong directional selection in which bacteria that are resistant to antibiotics are selected for and bacteria that are sensitive to antibiotics are selected against. This leaves physicians no option but to use stronger and more expensive antibiotics to cure bacterial infections. Some bacterial strains are now resistant to all available antibiotics, leading to a potentially serious public health crisis. A similar situation has occurred in some insect species, in which widespread use of **insecticides** has driven the evolution of insecticide resistance in these agricultural pests.

Disruptive Selection

Like directional selection, disruptive selection also favors extreme phenotypes. Both extremes, however, are favored (as opposed to just

Preventing Antibiotic Resistance

Penicillin, one of the first antibiotics identified, was hailed as a "miracle drug" when it was first used in the early 1940s. Killer diseases such as pneumonia (caused by the bacterium *Streptococcus pneumoniae*), wound infections (caused by *Staphylococcus aureus*), and gonorrhea (caused by *Neisseria gonorrhoeae*) were no match for it. Within a few years, however, some of the bacteria that cause these diseases developed a resistance to penicillin and then to other antibiotics. Today, these diseases and others are once more a serious threat to humans.

Antibacterial products such as hand soap, laundry detergent, and even toothpaste line supermarket shelves. It is unclear how much products like these may contribute to antibiotic resistance. To slow down the development of antibiotic resistance, the Mayo Clinic advises individuals to (1) take antibiotics exactly as prescribed, (2) never take antibiotics without a prescription, and (3) know when antibiotics can be useful and do not pressure doctors for antibiotics if you have an illness caused by a virus.

one), while intermediate phenotypes are selected against. Using the flower color example above, suppose that pollinators prefer red and white flowers over pink flowers. Natural selection acting in this situation will reduce the pink-flowered individuals and promote the occurrence of red- and white-flowered individuals.

Another example of disruptive selection involves beak size of the large cactus finch (*Geospiza conirostris*), a seed-eating bird in the Galápagos Islands. During drought years, plants produced either large or small seeds. Seeds of intermediate size were uncommon. Birds with large beaks were able to crack and eat large seeds. Birds with small beaks ate small seeds. Birds with intermediate beaks were unable to eat large or small seeds as effectively as other birds and were selected against because they could not acquire enough food resources. This produced a population of finches with large and small beaks. Similar instances of disruptive selection have been observed in other bird species.

Stabilizing Selection

Unlike directional or disruptive selection, stabilizing selection favors intermediate phenotypes and selects against extreme phenotypes. Stabilizing selection does not change the average value of traits. Instead, it narrows the range of traits expressed.

Stabilizing selection has been found in many species. Studies of various birds have found that very small or very large individuals have lower survival rates. Intermediate-size birds, however, have high survival rates. Human babies of intermediate size (between 7 and 8 pounds, or 3.2 and 3.6 kg) have significantly higher survival rates than infants that are extremely small (less than 4 pounds, or 1.8 kg) or extremely large (over 9 pounds, or 4.5 kg).

SELECTION AND SPECIATION

Darwin reasoned that separate populations of a species would differentiate if subjected to different selective pressures. That is, over long periods of time, individuals in these different populations would cease to breed with one another, and natural selection would lead to the formation of new species, a process called speciation. Inability to interbreed can be caused by a natural barrier such as a river or

mountain separating two populations. Barriers to successful reproduction can also occur during the process of mating, whether by
failure of gametes to unite or by failure of offspring to survive and
produce offspring of their own.

As species form, they can be envisioned as a lineage splitting and
diverging to form two lineages that eventually become separate species over time. Despite being different species, they still show some
similarities that reflect their common ancestry. The only figure Darwin included in *The Origin of Species* showed how this process could
occur. Modern evolutionary biologists continue to use this type of
tree-shaped figure (called a **dendrogram**) to show evolutionary relationships among species.

In the cases of the finches, tortoises, tree daisies, and other
species of the Galápagos Islands, Darwin concluded that ancestral
plants and animals colonized the islands from the South American
mainland. Because the Galápagos are volcanic islands that arose
from the ocean, they were uninhabited by other plants or animals
and all habitats and resources were available to be used. As the colonist species reproduced, their offspring and later descendents were
able to specialize in their use of the numerous available habitats and
resources.

ADAPTIVE RADIATION

The way an organism gathers and uses resources and interacts with
other organisms in the environment is called its **niche**, and each
species fills a particular niche. Thus, the descendents of the original
colonists became specialized in their ecological roles as they filled
all of the open, available niches on the islands. As they became more
specialized through natural selection, they gradually became different from one another and from the original colonists in both appearance and ecological function. Over time, they could successfully
breed only with other plants or animals that filled the same niche.
After long periods of time, this process gave rise to specialized species adapted to use their environment and its resources in specific
ways. This process of many new species arising from an original
colonist species and filling all the available niches is called **adaptive
radiation**.

Adaptive radiation occurs most frequently in oceanic islands. Many excellent examples of adaptive radiation are found in the Hawaiian Islands. The silverswords are a group of 30 species of plants in three different genera (*Argyroxiphium* spp., *Wilkesia* spp., and *Dubautia* spp.) found only in Hawaii. These beautiful plants evolved

Genetic Similarity

Modern evolutionary biologists use genetic data to evaluate evolutionary relationships among species. Based upon the laws of inheritance, DNA is passed from parents to offspring. Consequently, individuals that are closely related will have DNA that is more similar to each other than to individuals outside the immediate family. For example, brothers and sisters are genetically more similar to one another than they are to their cousins. The siblings' DNA is more similar because they share two recent common ancestors, their parents. They share a more distant common ancestor, a grandparent or grandparents, with their cousins. Thus, cousins are more genetically different, but still share some genetic similarities between them.

The same principle applies to species. Species that are genetically similar to one another share a recent common ancestor and consequently are more closely related than species that are quite genetically different from one another. For example, humans and chimpanzees share approximately 98% of their DNA. This indicates that they are two closely related species sharing a recent common ancestor. From the genetic differences, scientists estimate that humans and chimps split into separate lineages approximately 6 million years ago.

Humans and frogs are less genetically similar, indicating that they share a distant common ancestor. The similarities in their bodies and DNA, however, indicate that the lineage that gave rise to frogs and the lineage that gave rise to humans shared a common ancestor in the very distant past.

from ancestral species of plants called tarweeds that colonized Hawaii from the Pacific Coast of North America. The original tarweed colonists underwent adaptive radiation, and now the silverswords occupy all habitats in the Hawaiian Islands, from the highest to lowest elevations as well as the driest and wettest forests. Researchers have crossed various tarweeds and produced plants that are remarkably similar to the silverswords. Likewise, different species of fruit flies (*Drosophila* spp.), each with their own unique features and mating rituals, have evolved through a combination of natural selection and adaptive radiation in the Hawaiian Islands.

Another fascinating example of adaptive radiation is in a diverse group of fish called cichlids in Africa's Lake Victoria. The cichlid species of Lake Victoria come in a diversity of sizes and colors. Each species has unique adaptations that allow them to fill a multitude of niches in the lake. Some eat algae, some eat other fish, some eat insects, and some eat leaves. Genetic studies have shown that all cichlids in the lake are descended from a common ancestor that colonized Lake Victoria from the Nile River. In this habitat, cichlids

Specialization Has Its Risks

The specialization of species presents some of the most amazing examples of adaptation and evolution known. While specialization can allow use of a particular resource, however, problems can arise. If the resource is no longer available, a species dependent upon it can go extinct. This is particularly the case for many species on islands. Because they evolved on islands and are found nowhere else, they are highly vulnerable to extinction. Many native Hawaiian species are facing this problem today. These plants and animals have become so specialized in their habitat and resource needs through natural selection that as habitats are altered or destroyed by humans, they have nowhere else to go. Conservation efforts often seek to protect species whose specialization has left them vulnerable.

Figure 5.4 Members of the cactus family (*top*) are native to dry areas of North and South America, and have adapted spines and succulent stems in order to survive in arid climates. Some types of succulent euphorbs (*bottom*) have adapted similar characteristics, but are native to Africa and Madagascar. The traits of succulent cacti and euphorbs display convergent evolution.

diversified and evolved into more than 300 different species. Unfortunately, the introduction of the Nile tilapia (*Oreochromis niloticus*), which competes with the cichlids for resources, and predators such as the Nile perch (*Lates niloticus*) have driven many cichlid species in Lake Victoria to extinction.

CONVERGENT EVOLUTION

Another example of the power of natural selection can be seen in instances of **convergent evolution**. In convergent evolution, natural selection causes species in different lineages to evolve similar features in response to similar selection pressures. For example, the deserts of southwestern North America contain many different species of cacti, in the cactus family (the Cactaceae). These plants are adapted to the hot desert environment by having thick, fleshy stems that store water and leaves modified into protective spines. African deserts also contain plants that have fleshy, water-storing stems and protective spines. These plants, however, are in the spurge family (the Euphorbiaceae), which is vastly different from the cacti. Other examples of convergent evolution can be seen in comparisons between **marsupial mammals** in Australia and **placental mammals** found on the continents of Africa, Asia, Europe, and North and South America. Members of the separate marsupial and placental lineages that fill similar ecological niches share many similarities that allow them to perform the same ecological roles in their respective areas.

SUMMARY

Natural selection is a difference in survival or offspring production by individuals with different phenotypes. The measure of survival or reproductive output is called fitness. It is through natural selection and differences in fitness that adaptations spread and become established in a species. Natural selection can be directional, disruptive, or stabilizing, depending on the phenotype it favors. Natural selection can lead to the formation of new species in some instances. Many new species can be formed through the process of adaptive radiation, in which lineages diversify different structures. In contrast, natural selection can also drive convergent evolution, in which different lineages evolve similar features in response to common environmental pressures.

6

Sexual Selection

When the males and females of any animal have the same general habits of life, but differ in structure, colour, or ornament, such differences have been mainly caused by sexual selection.
—*Charles Darwin,* The Origin of Species

The crisp autumn is a time of great natural beauty in the Colorado Rocky Mountains. As the trees begin to change colors, herds of elk (*Cervus canadensis*) move from the high mountains into the open meadows. Once gathered, the males begin bugling, both to attract females and to indicate their presence to other males. While the bugling of the elks might not sound particularly musical to humans, it is irresistible to female elk, as are the impressive antlers the males have been growing since spring. The male that can attract and keep the most females will reproduce more and pass on more of his genes to later generations.

Males determine who the dominant male is by locking horns and conducting a form of ritualized wrestling in the presence of the females. These matches, which typically do not injure the males, determine who leads the herd. The winner of this contest, now established as the alpha male, attracts the most females and leaves more offspring, thereby passing on more of his DNA to future generations. Victory is fleeting, however. Eventually he will lose his status, and another male will take his place as leader of the herd.

REPRODUCTIVE SUCCESS

Reproduction is a critical component of the life cycle of any organism, and it is of the utmost importance that individuals breed with the best possible mate. In general, males need to demonstrate their superiority over other males. Because the male gamete, sperm, is energetically inexpensive to produce, males improve their fitness by mating with as many females as possible. In contrast, females have a limited amount of resources to dedicate to reproduction, and each individual offspring they produce represents a greater resource investment on the part of the female. Thus, females increase their fitness by producing high-quality offspring. Both males and females of any species attempt to ensure that their genes will be passed on successfully to future generations.

The fundamental forces behind evolutionary change through natural selection are differences in survival and reproduction among individuals. In many species of animals, and even some plants, differences in reproductive success can be caused by the choice of a mate or by competition among individuals for the opportunity to mate. This phenomenon of differences in reproductive success of individuals is a special case of natural selection identified by Darwin called **sexual selection**. Darwin recognized this unique phenomenon and described it as "a struggle between the individuals of one sex," and he said that the typical result "is not death to the unsuccessful competitor, but few or no offspring." Therefore, any traits that help an individual secure more mates will be passed on to its offspring, who as a result may themselves experience greater reproductive success.

INTRASEXUAL SELECTION IN ANIMALS

The most common form of sexual selection involves competition among members of the same sex, usually males, for access to and the opportunity to mate with members of the opposite sex. This form of sexual selection, known as **intrasexual selection**, can take many different forms. Some of the most well-known forms of intrasexual selection involve various forms of "combat" among males. A classic example can be seen in the head-butting competitions between male bighorn sheep (*Ovis canadensis*). In a series of ritualized combats, the males ram their heads together to establish their social status in the population. Those males that attain the highest social rank from these contests have access to the most females.

Other species such as deer, elk, and moose also utilize their horns in competitions for breeding status. Intense intrasexual selection among males has also been observed in other animals such as wolves (*Canis lupus*) and elephant seals (*Mirounga leonina* and *Mirounga angustirostris*) in which male combat dictates social rank and therefore the opportunity to breed. As individuals lose their rank, other males can potentially move up in the hierarchy of the group.

Intrasexual selection does not always involve fighting. In some species of birds and fish, males will use different behaviors such as vocalizing or physical displays to establish territories that will be used for breeding. Males that defend larger, higher-quality territories have more opportunities to mate with females. In bird species such as prairie chickens and sage grouse in North America and manakins, hummingbirds, and birds of paradise in the tropics, males will gather in groups at a particular location. This gathering of males in a breeding ground is called a **lek**. In the lek, males establish a social hierarchy based on various displays of feathers and vocalizations that allow them to establish and hold territories. The dominant males who defend the best territory attract the most females for mating.

INTERSEXUAL SELECTION IN ANIMALS

The lek mating behaviors described above involve not only intrasexual selection but also decisions by members of the opposite sex about which male to choose for mating. This situation is called **intersexual selection**, and it involves females making choices about males. In instances of intersexual selection, males may perform some type of ritualized courtship behavior, have a desirable trait, or defend a territory, and females evaluate these characteristics before making a decision about whether to mate with a particular male.

The courtship behavior of males can involve a number of different behaviors, such as displays of coloration, singing courtship songs, or performance of courtship dances. For example, consider the dramatic tail plumage of the Indian peafowl (*Pavo cristatus*). Males of this species (called peacocks) use their tail-feather display to attract

Figure 6.1   An example of intrasexual selection is combat by males. These big horn sheep are butting heads over a female (*left*).

females. Males with larger, more colorful tails that have more spots are preferred by females (called peahens) and consequently experience greater reproductive success than other males. Studies of different frog and bird species have also shown that males that sing longer, more complex songs attract more females and, therefore, have greater reproductive success than males who sing shorter, less complex songs.

One of the most striking examples of female choice in sexual selection is found in a group of birds in Australia and New Guinea called bowerbirds. There are numerous species of bowerbirds grouped in several related genera. One of the most thoroughly studied is the satin bowerbird (*Ptilonorhynchus violaceus*). Male bowerbirds begin their courtship by using twigs and grasses to build a small, covered platform called a bower. They decorate the bower with flowers, berries, feathers, string, and other colored objects. Interestingly, researchers have discovered blue items are most often chosen to decorate the bowers. Females visit the bower to observe the male as he performs an excited, frantic courtship dance called a buzz/wing-flip. In this dance, the male flaps and extends his wings, fluffs up his feathers, and makes a variety of buzzing vocalizations as he runs back and forth in front of the female. Females visit several bowers to observe the dances. After viewing the different males, the females return to one of the males' bowers to mate. After mating, the females leave to build a nest, where they will lay their eggs and raise their young.

While female bowerbirds tend to choose males with better-constructed bowers, their tastes change as they age. Young females prefer to mate with males whose bowers are more brightly decorated. Older females, however, care less about the bower's decorations. They make their choice based upon the quality of the males' dances. Researchers have concluded that the wild courtship dance startles young females and can drive them away. Older females, having already seen this bizarre behavior, are less startled by it. They prefer a male with a high-quality buzz/wing-flip.

DIFFERENCES IN APPEARANCE

One consequence of sexual selection is that it often results in dramatic differences in the appearance of the males and females of a species. For example, peacocks are brightly colored and have large tail plumage. Peahens have drab-colored plumage and lack the dramatic tails of the males. Similar differences between males and females can be found in numerous species of birds, from the common Northern cardinal (*Cardinalis cardinalis*) to the more exotic resplendent quetzal (*Pharomachrus mocinno*). Many other animals, including bighorn sheep, elk, lions, and even black widow spiders, exhibit similar differences between males and females. This dramatic difference in appearance between the males and females of a species is called **sexual dimorphism**. Coloration dimorphisms between males and females, particularly in birds, can also reflect additional selective differences between males and females. While males are under selection for brighter coloration to attract mates, drab coloration in females provides camouflage for them while they are sitting on the nest incubating eggs.

WHAT ARE FEMALES CHOOSING?

In both intersexual and intrasexual selection, the driving force is improved reproductive success. For intrasexual selection, it is obvious that the males who are able to win competitions or defend higher-quality territories are either stronger or more fit and therefore have better traits to pass on to their offspring. But for intersexual selection, the traits used in female choice need to indicate which male is the better mate. For example, a male elk's antlers not only help him

Figure 6.2 A male great bowerbird (*Chlamydera nuchalis*) displays in front of a female. The male collected the blue objects in front of the bower as part of his attempt at mating with the female.

Figure 6.3 Male elk have antlers, while females do not. This is an example of sexual dimorphism.

move up in rank in his herd, they may also protect him from predators. A male with large horns is more likely to have sons with large horns and, therefore, more surviving descendants. Thus, a large-horned male is often a better choice for a female. In contrast, other traits involved in female choice often have no apparent value and can even be somewhat of a detriment because they are produced at an energetic cost to the male. Researchers have asked why females would choose males with qualities such as these.

One answer to this situation is referred to as the **bright male** or **good genes hypothesis**. Under this hypothesis, females use traits such as bright plumage to indicate a male's overall health. Plumage color and brightness may indicate a male's ability to resist parasites or other diseases. Likewise, the health of a male could indicate his success at finding food. Individuals that are in poor health because of factors such as disease, parasites, or malnutrition will have duller coloration and therefore be less likely to attract the favorable attention of females. In contrast, the bright coloration of healthy males indicates better overall health, greater immunity to diseases, and/or better skills at finding food.

Studies of various bird and fish species support the bright male hypothesis. In different experiments, researchers have manipulated the coloration of individuals. In these experiments, researchers have changed the coloration of individuals by feeding them higher-quality diets, thus changing the coloration of beaks and feathers. Some researchers have even painted males to alter their appearance. In all of these experiments, the more brightly colored males were more successful than duller individuals at attracting mates.

Another explanation of the male traits that females use when choosing mates is called the **handicap hypothesis**. Here, the females make their choice based upon a trait that may present a survival risk to the males. Any male that can survive despite having such a trait must be superior to other males.

Many excellent examples of the handicap hypothesis can be found in studies of the long-tailed widowbird (*Euplectes progne*). Long-tailed widowbirds are one of several widowbird species that live in the open grasslands of Africa. During the nonbreeding season, both male and female widowbirds have a brownish or buff coloration that helps hide them in the grasses of the savannah where they live. During the breeding season, however, the males change their appearance drastically. First, they **molt**, and then they produce black feathers on most of their body. Males of different widowbird species may also produce bright red and/or yellow epaulets, collars, and chevrons on their body. They also produce black tail feathers that can be up to 20 inches (51 centimeters) long.

During the breeding season, males secure a territory and build multiple nest frames within it. Males with nesting territories tend to have redder epaulets than males without nesting territories, a clear example of intrasexual selection in this species. After building their nest frames, males perform a flight display that has a bouncy, rowing appearance with loops and exaggerated wing beats to attract females to their territory. When a female chooses a male, she lines one of the nest frames with fine grass before laying her eggs. Males do not share parenting duties. After the breeding season,

Figure 6.4 This male long-tailed widowbird in Natal, South Africa, displays its breeding plumage. When mating season is over, the male sheds its long and colorful feathers, assuming an appearance similar to that of the female.

males shed the black feathers and long tails, returning to their buff coloration.

Biologists wondered whether female long-tailed widowbirds preferred males with longer tails and whether males with longer tails fathered more offspring than males with shorter tails. To test whether tail length was important to females, biologists conducted a series of experiments. In the first stage of the experiments, researchers counted the number of nests maintained by a group of male long-tailed widowbirds. The more nests a male maintained, the more reproductively successful he was assumed to be. Next, the researchers manipulated the tail length of the male long-tailed widowbirds in their study group. Male birds were assigned to one of four experimental treatments. In the first group of males, tails were shortened. In the second group of males, tails were lengthened by gluing the feathers cut from the first group of males to their tail feathers. In the third group, tails were cut and then glued back onto the same male. In the fourth group, tails were not cut, allowing them to serve as a *control group*, or group in which the factor being tested is not applied for comparison purposes.

The researchers then monitored the males, counting the number of new nests that they established. Males whose tails were shortened had significantly fewer nests on average than males in the other three groups. Males whose tails were uncut or cut and glued back

Tail Length in Short-tailed Widowbirds

After studying sexual selection in long-tailed widowbirds, researchers wondered whether females of other widowbird species also preferred long-tailed males. To investigate this question, researchers conducted a similar tail manipulation experiment on the red-shouldered widowbird (*Euplectes axillaris*), a relatively short-tailed species. These females also preferred males with longer tails. Why, then, have tails remained short in this species? Several possible explanations, including lack of genetic variation for longer tails, high energetic costs of producing longer tails, and difficulty flying with longer tails, are being investigated as possible selective forces preventing evolution of increased tail length in this species.

on had the same number of nests as originally observed and were not different from one another. Males with the artificially lengthened tails had the greatest number of nests. This experiment clearly demonstrates that tail length is an important trait in long-tailed widowbirds. The researchers, however, did not test whether the longer-tailed males experienced greater mortality as a result of having longer tails. An experiment investigating this phenomenon would determine whether the benefit of a long tail comes at a survival cost. If so, this would be an interesting confirmation of stabilizing selection acting in this species.

A final hypothesis regarding female choice is called the **resource hypothesis**, which proposes that females choose males who will provide the best resources. In some species, the male makes this obvious by giving a **nuptial gift** to the female. For example, in a number of insect species, males offer food to the female to get her to choose him for a mate. The gifts range from seeds to balls of dung. The dance fly (*Rhamphomyia sulcata*) male captures a prey item and wraps it in silk before presenting it to the female. If she accepts it, they mate. Some males cheat the system by offering females empty balls of silk.

In cases where males defend a territory, those males with better territories should be able to provide better food resources to the female. It is unclear, however, whether the female is attracted to the male himself or just to his territory. Either way, a male that can offer a female more food is the best choice.

SEXUAL SELECTION IN PLANTS

Plants clearly cannot compete directly, and, of course, females cannot consciously choose a mate. There is, however, evidence of sexual selection in these organisms, particularly in flowering plants.

In a majority of flowering plants, flowers contain both male and female structures. A plant's success as a male depends on its ability to pollinate and fertilize flowers on other plants. Plants that attract more pollinators should donate more pollen and fertilize more eggs. Studies of plant reproduction have shown that pollinators prefer larger individual flowers and larger displays of multiple flowers over smaller ones. Male plants that produce larger floral displays outcompete males that produce smaller flowers or smaller floral displays.

After pollen is deposited on the stigma (the receptive female structure in a flower), pollen grains germinate and grow through the **style** toward the **ovary,** where they fertilize the eggs. Researchers have investigated whether pollen tubes compete with one another by racing through the style toward the eggs. In essence, these studies are testing whether faster-growing pollen grains will produce stronger offspring. Researchers have compared the outcome of situations

Darwin's Mystery Pollinator

Many flowering plants depend on animal pollinators to transport pollen from one plant to another. This gives pollinators the potential to be a strong selective force when it comes to shaping the traits of flowers. For example, different pollinators prefer different colors. Bees prefer yellow, blue, and purple flowers. Birds prefer bright red and orange flowers. Bats and moths prefer white flowers, which are easier to see at night. Pollinators are also attracted to plants that offer them pollen or nectar to eat. A plant that uses color and food rewards effectively will attract more pollinators and thus experience greater reproductive success. In addition to attracting pollinators, plants must also guard their rewards so that only good pollinators receive them.

The relationship between plant and pollinator can become so close that only one pollinator can access the reward and successfully transport pollen. Darwin recognized this relationship when he studied the Madagascar star orchid, also called Darwin's orchid (*Angraecum sesquipedale*). This plant holds nectar at the base of a tube that is up to 12 inches (30 cm) long. Although the pollinator was unknown at the time, Darwin predicted that it must be an insect with mouth parts long enough to reach the nectar. Biologists thought Darwin's prediction was foolhardy until in which a large number of pollen grains are deposited on stigmas with situations in which a low number of pollen grains are deposited on a stigma. The results of these studies have shown that in high-competition instances where there are a large number of pollen grains competing to fertilize the eggs, the offspring produced grow with greater vigor than in low-competition instances where there are fewer pollen grains present. These results support the conclusion that there is a benefit to strong competition in plants. Further studies, however, are needed to appreciate fully this phenomenon

Figure 6.5 Darwin was able to support his theories of evolution using this species of orchid (*left*). The hawkmoth (*right*), the orchids' sole pollinator, developed long feeding parts so that it could successfully drink nectar from the similarly long orchid.

the hawkmoth *Xanthophan morgani praedicta* was discovered 40 years later. Its strawlike mouth parts, which it unrolls to feed, are 10 to 14 inches (25 to 36 cm) long. Close relationships such as this, in which traits of one species shape the evolution of another and vice versa, are known as **coevolution**.

of apparent male competition and intersexual selection in plant reproduction.

One aspect of pollen-tube competition is that even if pollen from one plant has slower growth than pollen from a different plant, the slower-growing pollen can still fertilize eggs by arriving on the stigma and germinating before the faster-growing pollen grain arrives. In at least one plant species, however, the female balances the playing field. In Menges' fameflower (*Phemeranthus mengesii*), the stigma contains chemicals that prevent pollen-grain germination. After the flower has been open for awhile and collected pollen from several different males, the chemicals wear off, allowing all pollen grains to germinate at the same time. This gives all individuals an equal chance to fertilize the eggs.

SUMMARY

Sexual selection is a special form of natural selection. In one form of sexual selection called intrasexual selection, males compete with one another to establish rank and to gain access to females for mating. This male competition can involve horns or other elaborate structures that are used for ritualized combat or impressive displays. In the other form of sexual selection, intersexual selection, females rely on a variety of features such as coloration, courtship dances, and nuptial gifts to evaluate potential mates. Sexual selection is more obvious in animals, but it also occurs in plants.

Objections to Darwin's Theory

*Remember, the greatest discovery ever made by man, namely,
the law of the attraction of gravity, was also attacked.*
—*Charles Darwin,* The Origin of Species

From July 10 through July 21, 1925, a series of events unfolded in the small town of Dayton, Tennessee, that will always be remembered for their incredible effect on science and science education in the United States. During these 12 days, the state of Tennessee tried John Scopes for teaching evolution in his classroom. In March of that year, the Tennessee Legislature passed a law called the Butler Act that made it illegal for any teacher in the state "to teach any theory that denies the story of the Divine Creation of man as taught in the Bible, and to teach instead that man has descended from a lower order of animals." Scopes was arrested and charged with teaching evolution on May 7, 1925. This was the beginning of "The Scopes Monkey Trial."

The trial was more about publicity than anything. The American Civil Liberties Union had offered to pay for the defense of anyone willing to stand trial for breaking the Butler Act. As soon as the Butler Act was passed, a group of Dayton businesspeople discussed the possibility of a trial to bring money and publicity to their town. They

Figure 7.1 The Scopes trial took place at the Rhea County Courthouse in Dayton, Tennessee, on July 17, 1925. In this photo, Judge John T. Raulston of Winchester, Tennessee, is about to deliver the decision in the case.

convinced John Scopes, a substitute science teacher and football coach at the local school, to allow himself to be arrested for teaching the evolution section in the state-approved science book, *Hunter's Civic Biology*.

At first the conspirators tried to get the English science-fiction writer H.G. Wells to serve as the defense attorney, but he declined. Eventually, Clarence Darrow, a well-known intellectual and agnostic, agreed to lead the defense. William Jennings Bryan, a famous orator, politician, and religious fundamentalist, was chosen to lead the prosecution. Judge John T. Raulston presided over the proceedings.

For 12 days, Dayton was a carnival of protesters, reporters, and gawkers. Radio announcers provided the first-ever live broadcasts from a court trial. Expert witnesses on science and religion provided testimony. The high point of the trial came when Darrow called Bryan to the stand to serve as an expert on religion. Darrow's cross-examination is famous for its intense questioning that left Bryan confused and unable to answer coherently. Nevertheless, the jury returned a verdict of guilty, and Scopes was fined $100.

In January 1927, the Tennessee Supreme Court overturned the guilty verdict on a technicality, and then dismissed the charges. Despite the drama and emotion on both sides, the trial accomplished very little. It was, however, a watershed event in the history of science education in general and the teaching of evolution in particular.

EARLY CRITICISMS OF DARWIN AND NATURAL SELECTION

The Scopes Monkey Trial was not the first time the theories of natural selection and evolution had come under attack. Upon publication of *The Origin of Species*, Darwin and his ideas were vehemently attacked in sermons and satirized in caricatures. As soon as Darwin presented his theory, others tried to counter it. The fossil records that Darwin used to illustrate the progression of life on Earth were interpreted by some as evidence of the great biblical Noachian flood. This interpretation, however, does not fit scientific facts. The rocks show a clear progression over geologic time from simple organisms in the lower, older layers to more complex forms in the higher, younger layers. With a flood, one would expect to find a mixture of fossils from all creatures in the various rock layers. Furthermore, geology shows that the rock layers were formed over millions of years and encase the fossilized remains of life from different times in Earth's history rather than being formed instantly in one great flood event.

MR. BERGH TO THE RESCUE.

THE DEFRAUDED GORILLA. "That *Man* wants to claim my Pedigree. He says he is one of my Descendants."

MR. BERGH. "Now, Mr. DARWIN, how could you insult him so?"

Figure 7.2 This Victorian cartoon depicts a gorilla asking Henry Bergh, founder of the American Society for the Prevention of Cruelty to Animals, to defend him against Darwin's claims that they are related.

SCIENTIFIC CREATIONISM AND INTELLIGENT DESIGN

In response to such clear evidence presented by the biological sciences, some have proposed alternative explanations to evolution, such as **scientific creationism** or its more recent incarnation, **intelligent design**. There is nothing scientific about scientific creationism.

Figure 7.3 The *Archaeopteryx* fossil, found in 1862, shows a combination of lizard and bird features. This fossil is widely credited as the first missing link fossil.

While science proposes hypotheses and performs experiments to test them, scientific creationism depends on assumptions that are either not testable or are known to be scientifically incorrect. For

Figure 7.4 The *Tiktaalik* is another missing link organism, thought to be a transition between fish and four-legged organisms, including all mammals, reptiles, birds, and amphibians. The first *Tiktaalik* fossil was found in northern Canada in 2006.

example, scientific creationism cites as evidence of creation by a deity the "fact" that there are no transitional forms of life, no **missing links** in the fossil record. This is simply not true.

Paleontologists found the first missing-link fossil in 1862. It had the bones, tail, teeth, and claws of a lizard and the feathers of a bird. They named the fossil *Archaeopteryx*, meaning "ancient wing." The layers of rock in which it was found indicate that it lived during the Jurassic period 150 million to 155 million years ago. The combination of lizard and bird features clearly indicates a transitional form between lizards and birds. This, coupled with the fact that modern birds and reptiles share many genetic similarities, has led evolutionary biologists to conclude that birds evolved from an early reptile ancestor.

There are fossils in China, Russia, North America, and Greenland that show different steps in the evolution of fish ancestors whose fins underwent progressive changes to form legs. Fish with such mutations would have had a distinct survival advantage in being able to escape pools that dried up. These fossils also show changes in the rib cage and body cavity necessary for support when these organisms left the water.

In 2006, researchers in Canada found a fossilized creature called *Tiktaalik* (meaning "large, shallow-water fish"). The fossil shows an

Making Fossils

It is important to remember that fossils will form only under specific conditions, such as the low-oxygen mud of swamps and lake beds or the dry sand dunes of deserts. Fossils will preserve only hard tissues such as shells and bone. Soft tissues such as muscles and organs do not fossilize. Neither do behavioral traits or physiological adaptations that can play a major role in survival and fitness. Thus, scientists must use the information that is available in fossils, interpreting it based on comparisons with living animals and plants. Far from being incomplete, paleontologists actually have a rich and highly informative fossil record that shows the changes in organisms over the history of life on Earth.

interesting mixture of structures. *Tiktaalik* has the jaw, scales, fins, and gill structures of a fish and the ribs, neck, and skull structures of a four-legged land animal (called a **tetrapod**). This intermediate fish/tetrapod ancestor lived approximately 375 million years ago, when the area that is now Canada was closer to the equator and had a tropical climate.

Recent attempts to teach scientific creationism alongside biology have failed because it has been shown that "creation science" is not science at all. More recently, however, scientific creationism has evolved into a new form called intelligent design, or ID, which has been proposed as an alternative to evolution and natural selection. Intelligent design proposes that living organisms are so complex that natural selection and evolution could not possibly have produced them; ergo, there must have been an intelligent designer. This is basically a modern variant of an argument set forth by the British philosopher William Paley (1743–1805), who said that the intricate mechanisms of a watch are obviously the work of an intelligent designer. Paley argued that if one investigates living organisms in the same way, the complexity of the interacting parts automatically indicates an intelligent designer.

This analogy, still used by ID proponents, is flawed on several counts. First, watches are very different from living organisms. While the complexity of a watch needs to be planned and assembled, organismal complexity has arisen from a series of progressive, inherited changes in which new parts are developed and accumulated in different types of living things. Over long periods, selection and other evolutionary processes refine, improve, accumulate, and diversify components of life-forms to produce the diversity of life seen today.

Another flaw in the ID argument is the claim that just as a watch will not work without all of the parts assembled in the appropriate way, complex biological structures will also fail to function if one part is not there; as a result, complex structures could not have evolved from simpler structures. This concept is called **irreducible complexity**. A classic example used by ID proponents is the bacterial **flagellum**, a whiplike structure that some bacteria use to propel themselves. ID proponents argue that a flagellum is composed of many different parts that have no function except as part of the flagellum. While it is true that the bacterial flagellum has many parts, it is not true that they have no other function. Researchers have shown that the different components of the flagellum are actually found in

Not So Intelligent Design

There are many interesting examples of amazing and seemingly perfect adaptation. That, however, does not necessarily mean they were designed by an intelligent force. While examples of perfect design receive a great deal of attention from proponents of intelligent design, there are many examples of designs that are less than perfect. The human eye, for example, has a **blind spot** where the optic nerve passes through the **retina**. To test this, draw an X on one end of a note card and a dot on the other. Hold the card in front of your face at arm's length with the X on the right and the dot on the left. With the right eye closed, look at the X with your left eye. Slowly move the card toward your face. The dot will disappear, and then reappear as the card moves closer. Instead of seeing a hole where the blind spot loses the image, the brain fills in the gap with what it thinks should be there. Turn the card over and try again with the left eye closed and right eye open. Now, repeat this experiment, but this time draw a line through the dot. Although the dot will disappear, the line will not disappear because again the brain will fill in the blind spot with what it thinks should be there. The blind spot is an artifact from the process of eye development in earlier animals that natural selection and evolution failed to eliminate. It is a glitch that an intelligent designer would have eliminated in the first round of production.

other bacteria, which use them for different functions. For example, some bacteria use individual components for attaching to surfaces, while others use parts for nutrient uptake. In bacteria with this type of flagellum, the different parts have been combined in a new way for a new function—movement. Still other bacteria use a flagellum that is assembled in a completely different way using different parts. Thus, there is more than one way to assemble a bacterial flagellum, and they are not irreducibly complex.

Irreducible complexity has also been proposed for the clotting reactions of mammalian blood. Just as with the bacterial flagella, however, the components of blood that produce the clotting response in mammals are also found in other kinds of organisms. In mammals, the same basic parts have been combined in new ways to produce clotting in response to injury. This improved ability to heal obviously has high survival and adaptive value.

Similar examples can be found in plants. The many different genes and proteins required to stimulate flowering are actually just new combinations of those found in simpler, nonflowering plants. Thus, the fundamental ideas behind irreducible complexity are incorrect and have been proven false regarding a number of different phenomena in a wide variety of species.

HOMOLOGY

Natural selection can drive tremendous changes in a number of different structural features in plants and animals. Comparison of these structures among species is the basis of **comparative anatomy**. Such studies have shown that many similar structures show homology, indicating that they have been "reworked" through evolution to achieve different functions in different species. For example, the forelimbs of a human, dog, bat, horse, and whale are composed of the same bones. These bones, however, have been modified over time via mutation and natural selection so that now they function in very different ways. This shows how natural selection acting in conjunction with modifications of genetically controlled developmental processes can remodel common structures to achieve different results.

THE DOVER CASE

The teaching of ID as a scientific equivalent to natural selection was tested in 2005 in the case of *Tammy Kitzmiller, et al. v. Dover Area*

Forelimb Bone Homology

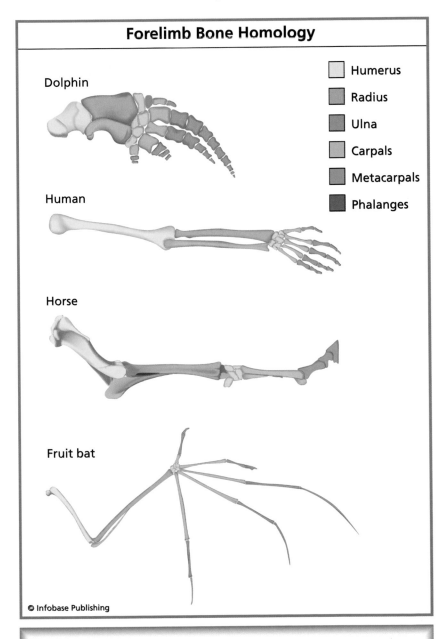

Dolphin

Human

Horse

Fruit bat

- Humerus
- Radius
- Ulna
- Carpals
- Metacarpals
- Phalanges

© Infobase Publishing

Figure 7.5 The forelimbs of the dolphin, horse, bat, and human show homology, or similarities of structure across different species.

Hox and MADS Genes

Recent advances in genetics and molecular biology have allowed researchers to investigate how certain genes modify developmental processes in different species to produce a wide array of different body shapes and parts. In animals, groups of genes called **Hox genes** regulate developmental processes in different regions of the body. For example, similar genes regulate development in the same region of the body in flies, mammals, birds, and snakes. Modifications of how these genes are expressed and regulated appear to be the cause for the differences among these different kinds of animals. Similarly, in plants, genes called **MADS genes** control development of reproductive structures. MADS genes control the development of cones in plants such as pines and spruces, while modifications of the expression of these genes produce flowers and their respective parts in flowering plants. Natural selection and evolution do not need to produce structures from scratch. Through evolutionary tinkering they can find new uses for existing parts.

School District, et al. Several groups of parents sued the Dover Area School District in Pennsylvania over attempts to have teachers read a statement to students that evolution is not a fact and that intelligent design is an acceptable alternative scientific theory. Members of the school board who opposed the statement resigned their positions, and science teachers protested the statement as a violation of professional standards. Eventually, parents filed their case against the school district.

The trial began September 26, 2005, and was presided over by Judge John E. Jones III. Both sides presented expert witnesses throughout the trial, which lasted until early November. Jones issued his decision on December 20, 2005, stating that intelligent design was not a scientific theory and could not be taught as such. He further stated that the evidence presented in the trial "established that ID is a religious view, a mere re-labeling of creationism, and not a scientific theory." Thus, the attempt to teach ID in the science classrooms of the Dover Area schools was stopped. Similar attempts in other areas have also been foiled.

QUESTIONS ABOUT NATURAL SELECTION AND EVOLUTION

Darwin's theory is definitely thought provoking. Some of the main questions and comments about the strength of natural selection and evolution are addressed below.

Evolution is an outdated idea that scientists are now rejecting. Actually, a vast majority of biologists accept natural selection and evolution as one of the two unifying principles of biology. Genetics is the other. Biologists do disagree about evolution,

Science Education Disclaimers

Similar to the Dover case, attempts have been made in other school districts to discredit natural selection and evolution. Several school systems have attempted to place disclaimer stickers in science textbooks. In one famous case, the Cobb County, Georgia, school system added stickers that read, "This textbook contains material on evolution. Evolution is a theory, not a fact, regarding the origin of living things. This material should be approached with an open mind, studied carefully, and critically considered." Clearly, the writers of the disclaimer stickers misinterpreted the scientific meaning of *theory*. As in the Dover case, judges did not allow these stickers to remain in books. It is interesting that no other established scientific theory has been the subject of so many attempts to discredit it since Galileo Galilei (1564–1642) provided proof of the theory developed by Nicolaus Copernicus (1473–1543) that the Sun (not the Earth) is the center of the solar system.

but the disagreements focus on *how* evolution happens, not *whether* evolution happens. For example, one issue in evolutionary biology that was hotly debated for a time was how quickly evolutionary change happens. Darwin suggested that evolutionary change is always gradual. Rapid evolutionary change, or **punctuated equilibrium**, however, has been shown to occur in other instances. After much debate and further study, evolutionary biologists found that both slow and rapid change probably take place at different times and in different organisms. This scientific disagreement highlights a strength of biology and scientific theories. When new perspectives and theories are presented, they are tested, investigated, and, if supported, incorporated into current theories.

Evolution is not a fact, but a theory that cannot be tested or proved. As discussed previously, scientists use the term *theory* differently from the general public. The concepts encompassed by the theories of natural selection and evolution have been tested and supported in many scientific studies investigating everything from fossils to DNA to animal behavior. The results of these studies all point to the same thing: that life on Earth has been subject to natural selection and that evolution has occurred.

Evolution cannot be observed, so it is a belief, not science. It is true that science depends on observation, but observations do not have to be direct for science to be valid. Experiments can be conducted based upon predictions of what should happen if the theory and assumptions of the experiment are correct. For example, the scientific fields of chemistry and physics are themselves largely based on the study of events and forces that cannot be directly observed. These sciences, like biology, must sometimes depend on indirect evidence to study certain phenomena.

Evolution is impossible because the occurrence of life-forms as different as elephants, cottonwood trees, butterflies, and bacteria is highly improbable. It is true that the evolution of any species represents the outcome of many random events. Improbable and impossible, however, are two different things. For example, imagine a room with five people, each with a different birthday. The probability that each person would have any particular birthday during the year is $^1/_{365}$ (0.0027%). The probability of five people being in a room with those five different birthdays is $^1/_{365} \times {}^1/_{365} \times {}^1/_{365}$

$\times$ $^1/_{365}$ $\times$ $^1/_{365}$, which equals 0.00000000000015%, a highly improbable event. Therefore, while it is improbable, the possibility of five people with those birthdays being in the same room is definitely not impossible.

Furthermore, if this experiment took place over a very long period of time with periodic selections of different groups of five people, the improbability would decrease even further. In evolution, small changes can add up to result in new and very different structures. What might seem improbable becomes simply difficult and much less unlikely. It is this part of evolution that most ID proponents do not include in their arguments.

If someone believes in evolution, they cannot have religious beliefs. This is absolutely not true. Natural selection, evolution, and science in general seek to explain phenomena in the natural world. They are not intended to explain everything in the human experience. Morals, ethics, and other aspects of human culture are topics of personal choice and conviction and are not addressed by science, nor are they within the realm of what science can explain. Darwin himself had strong religious convictions, as do many scientists who study evolution today. As the famous evolutionary biologist Stephen Jay Gould (1941–2002) expressed in many of his writings, science and religion address different aspects of being human that are not in conflict with one another. The idea that they are in conflict is a misunderstanding of both.

FINAL THOUGHTS

The study of natural selection and evolutionary biology are exciting fields of scientific inquiry. They investigate and test a number of intriguing questions about the story of life on Earth. An understanding of these topics is essential to a complete knowledge of modern biology. Furthermore, as scientists attempt to address climate change, protect endangered species, feed a hungry world, and protect people from disease, they must understand the fundamental roles of natural selection and evolution in life on Earth. Darwin understood that his ideas would have impacts beyond the laboratory, and that is why he so meticulously developed his evidence and arguments.

Darwin also realized, however, that his work would eventually have a tremendous positive impact on biology and science. It was, no doubt, with this appreciation for how his work would influence the study of biology that he wrote in the final chapter of *The Origin of Species*, "I look with confidence to the future, to young and rising naturalists."

Glossary

Adaptations   Traits or features of an organism that help it survive in its environment.

Adaptive radiation   The process of many new species arising from an original colonist species and filling all the available niches.

Alleles   Different forms of a gene that can be symbolized using letters such as *A* and *a*.

Antibiotic resistance   The ability of bacteria to evolve resistance to substances that previously had the capacity to kill or inhibit them.

Archaeopteryx   ("ancient wing") The first true missing-link fossil. It had the bones, tail, teeth, and claws of a lizard and the feathers of a bird.

Archipelago   A chain of oceanic islands.

Artificial selection   The process in which humans choose and mate plants and animals that have desired traits.

Binomial   A two-part scientific name for species, composed of genus and species.

Biogeography   The distribution of different kinds of plants and animals throughout the Earth.

Blind spot   A region in the visual field where there are no light receptors because of the optic nerve passing through the retina.

Breed   A specific type of animal or plant that has been selectively bred to have characteristic traits that are passed on to offspring.

Bright male hypothesis   An explanation for sexual selection that states females will choose males with brighter, more vibrant coloration because that will be a better indicator of the male's overall health.

Chromosomes   Long threads of DNA that carry genes in a linear sequence.

Codominance   The condition of two or more alleles being equally dominant, such as that which occurs in the human ABO blood groups.

Coevolution   Evolution between two unrelated but interdependent species in which change in one species causes change in the other species.

Comparative anatomy   The study of similarities and differences in the structure of different organisms.

Convergent evolution   When natural selection causes species in different lineages to evolve similar features in response to similar selection pressures.

Data   Information gathered by experimentation or observation.

Dendrogram   A figure showing evolutionary relationships among species.

deoxyribonucleic acid (DNA)   The inherited material composing chromosomes and containing the information of life.

Descent with modification   A phrase used by Darwin to describe subtle, gradual changes in characteristics from ancestors to descendents.

Directional selection   The condition in which one extreme phenotype is favored over the opposite extreme.

Disruptive selection   The condition in which both extreme phenotypes are favored, while intermediate phenotypes are selected against.

Domesticated   Tamed animal and plant species that have been changed through selective breeding by humans.

Dominant   An allele that is expressed and masks the expression of a recessive allele.

Environment   The combination of all external factors that can affect an organism.

Epithet   The second part of a two-part scientific name for species.

Evolution   Changes in allele frequencies within a population over time; also the change in a species over time.

F$_1$ generation   The first generation of offspring resulting from a mating.

F$_2$ generation   The second generation of offspring resulting from a mating.

Fitness   The measure of survival and reproductive success among individuals.

Flagellum   A whiplike structure that some bacteria use to propel themselves.

Fossils   The remains or impressions of organisms from previous geological ages.

Gemmules   Nonexistent particles once believed to combine during mating and to contain information needed to form offspring.

Gene   The basic functional unit that controls traits.

Genetics   The study of genes and heredity.

Genetic drift   Random changes in allele frequencies within small populations without the action of natural selection.

Genotype   The combination of alleles within an individual.

Genus   The first part of a two-part scientific name for species.

Glyptodont   A giant ancestor of modern armadillos, now extinct.

Good genes hypothesis   The idea in sexual selection that females choose males with better traits because those traits indicate better genes in the male.

Handicap hypothesis   The idea in sexual selection that some exaggerated traits in males are a detriment to the male. Therefore, if the male can survive with that trait, he is clearly a superior potential mate.

Hardy-Weinberg principle   A model that explains how one can predict the genotype frequencies in a population if one knows the allele frequencies in the population. Frequencies will not change if there is no evolution occurring in the population.

Heritability   The ability of traits to be passed from parents to offspring.

Heterozygous   A genotype in which the two alleles are different.

Homology   Similar characteristics in species descended from a common ancestor.

Homozygous   A genotype in which the two alleles are the same.

Hox genes   In animals, genes that regulate developmental processes in different regions of the body.

Hybrid   An offspring of two animal breeds or two plant varieties.

Hypothesis   A statement that makes a testable prediction to explain an observation.

Incomplete dominance   A situation in which neither allele is dominant to the other and instead the individual expresses an intermediate phenotype between the two extremes.

Industrial melanism   The evolution of dark coloration in moths inhabiting heavily polluted areas.

Insecticide   A substance used to kill insects.

Intelligent design   A belief that living organisms were produced by an intelligent designer because they are so complex that natural selection and evolution could not possibly have produced them.

Intersexual selection   Sexual selection in which individuals of one sex choose potential mates from members of the opposite sex.

Intrasexual selection   Sexual selection in which individuals of one sex compete for the opportunity to mate with members of the opposite sex.

Irreducible complexity   A flawed concept proposed by supporters of intelligent design that organismal traits are so complex that they could not have evolved from simpler forms.

Law of independent assortment   Also called the second law of inheritance. It states that different traits segregate independently of one another. It holds true only for traits that are controlled by genes found on different chromosomes.

Law of segregation   Also called the first law of heredity. It states that different alleles separate during gamete formation in the parents and are joined together in the offspring.

Lek   A breeding area used in some bird species in which male birds display for dominance among other males and opportunity to breed with females.

Lineage   The relatedness of the descendants of a particular ancestor.

Linked traits   Traits controlled by genes on the same chromosome.

MADS genes   In plants, genes that control development of reproductive structures.

Marsupial mammals   Animals in which the mother develops the young in a pouch; many species are native to Australia.

Mendelian inheritance   Inheritance of traits according to the principles and probabilities discovered and described by Gregor Mendel.

Missing links   An evolutionary transitional form of an organism between a primitive and advanced form.

Modern synthesis   The combination of Darwinian and Mendelian principles.

Molt   The process in which birds lose and replace their feathers.

Mutation   Changes in genetic material (DNA) that can create new alleles.

Natural selection   The process through which some individuals of a species have traits that allow them to survive and produce more offspring than others of their species.

Niche   The way an organism gathers and uses resources and interacts with other organisms in the environment.

Non-Mendelian inheritance   The inheritance of traits that does not conform to the principles and probabilities discovered and described by Gregor Mendel.

Nuptial gift   An item presented by a male to a female to entice her to mate with him.

Ovary   The structure in females where eggs are formed.

Paleontologist   A scientist who studies prehistoric life-forms.

Phenotype   An organism's observable features.

Placental mammals   Mammals in which young develop inside the mother; common on the continents of Africa, Asia, Europe, and North and South America.

Polled   A naturally hornless animal belonging to a normally horned species.

Pollen   A plant structure containing the male gamete, or sperm.

Pollinators   Animals that move pollen from one plant to another.

Population   A group of individuals of one species living in an area at the same time.

Punctuated equilibrium   A scientific theory that proposed that evolutionary changes can occur rapidly.

Race   A group of distinct yet closely related members of the same species.

Recessive   An allele whose expression is masked in the presence of a dominant allele.

Resource hypothesis   An idea in sexual selection that females will choose the males that can provide the best resources.

Retina   The light-sensing structure in the eye.

Scientific creationism   An idea developed in the attempt to find scientific evidence to support creation of life by a deity.

Scientific method   A clearly defined approach to investigating natural phenomena using observation, questioning, hypothesis, experimentation, data collection, and evaluation.

Scientific theory   An all-encompassing explanation of many well-supported observations and facts that explain a natural phenomenon.

Selective breeding   Artificial selection by which humans decide which plants or animals pass traits on to their offspring.

Sexual dimorphism   The condition in some species in which there is an obvious difference in structure or coloration between males and females.

Sexual selection   The special case of natural selection in which males and females compete for or choose mates.

Speciation   The process whereby a lineage of a new species forms by branching off from an original species.

Species   Organisms belonging to a group of populations that can interbreed.

Stabilizing selection   The condition in which intermediate phenotypes are selected for, while extreme phenotypes are selected against. It does not change the average value of traits but narrows the range of traits expressed.

Stigma   A female plant reproductive structure where the pollen germinates and guides the sperm to the female gamete, or egg.

Style   The structure of a flower that pollen grows through to deliver sperm to the egg.

Subspecies   A distinct grouping of organisms below the species levels, or within a species.

Teosinte   An ancestor of modern corn.

Tetrapod   A four-legged animal.

Theory of particulate inheritance   The theory developed by Gregor Mendel describing how specific particles (now known as genes) are passed from parent to offspring.

Tiktaalik   ("large, shallow-water fish") A fossil showing the jaw, scales, fins, and gill structures of a fish and the ribs, neck, and skull structures of a four-legged land animal.

Transmutation   The name Darwin first gave to the change that species undergo over time.

True-breeding   Organisms that consistently produce a trait from parent to offspring.

Varieties   See breed.

Wallace Line   The boundary separating the Asian and Australian zones of species.

Bibliography

Andersson, M. "Female Choice Selects for Extreme Tail Length in a Widowbird." *Nature* 299 (1982): 818–820.

Broad, W.J. "Useful Mutants Bred with Radiation." *New York Times* (August 28, 2007).

Burditt, L., U. Desilva, and J. Fitch. "Breeds of Livestock," Oklahoma State University Department of Animal Science Web site. Available online. URL: http://www.ansi.okstate.edu/breeds/.

Centers for Disease Control and Prevention. "Antibiotic/Antimicrobial Resistance," Centers for Disease Control and Prevention Web site. Available online. URL: http://www.cdc.gov/drugresistance/.

Darwin, C.R. *On the Origin of Species: By Means of Natural Selection or the Preservation of Favoured Races in the Struggle for Life.* New York: Penguin Books USA, 1958.

Darwin, C.R. *The Voyage of the* Beagle. New York: Penguin Classics, 1989.

Futuyma, D.J. *Evolution.* Sunderland, Mass.: Sinauer Associates, 2005.

Leff, D. "AboutDarwin.com. Dedicated to the Life and Times of Charles Darwin," About Darwin Web site. Available online. URL: http://www.aboutdarwin.com/index.html.

Nielsen, L.R. "Molecular Differentiation Within and Among Island Populations of the Endemic Plant *Scalesia affinis* (Asteraceae) from the Galapagos Islands." *Heredity* 93 (2004): 434–442.

Price, P.W. *Biological Evolution.* New York: Saunders College, 1996.

Pryke, S.R., and S. Andersson. "A Generalized Female Bias for Long Tails in a Short-tailed Widowbird." *Proceedings of the Royal Society of London B* 269 (2002): 2141–2146.

Pryke, S.R., S. Andersson, and M.J. Lawes. "Sexual Selection of Multiple Handicaps in the Red-collared Widowbird: Female Choice of Tail Length but Not Carotenoid Display." *Evolution* 55 (2001): 1452–1463.

Quammen, D. "Was Darwin Wrong?" *National Geographic* 206 (November 2004): 2–35.

Rennie, J. "15 Answers to Creationist Nonsense." *Scientific American* 287 (2002): 78–85.

Ritchie, H. "Harlan Ritchie's Beef Review," Michigan State University Department of Animal Science Web site. Available online. URL: http://www.msu.edu/~ritchieh/.

Rose, M.R., and L.D. Mueller. *Evolution and Ecology of the Organism.* Upper Saddle River, N.J.: Pearson Prentice Hall, 2006.

Trut, L.N. "Early Canid Domestication: The Farm-fox Experiment." *American Scientist* 87 (1999): 160–169.

Zimmer, C. "A Fin Is a Limb Is a Wing. How Evolution Fashioned Its Masterworks." *National Geographic* 210 (November 2006): 1110–1135.

Further Resources

Fitter, J., D. Fitter, and D. Hosking. *Wildlife of the Galapagos*. London: Collins, 2007.

Gamlin, L., *Eyewitness: Evolution.* New York: Dorling Kindersley, 2000.

Gibson, J.P., and T.R. Gibson. *Plant Diversity*. New York: Chelsea House, 2007.

Gonick, L., and A. Outwater. *The Cartoon Guide to the Environment*, New York: Collins, 1996.

Gonick, L., and M. Wheelis. *The Cartoon Guide to Genetics*. New York: Collins, 1991.

Grady D. *New York Times Deadly Invaders: Virus Outbreaks Around the World, from Marburn Fever to Avian Flu*. New York: Kingfisher, 2006.

Hopkinson, D., and N. Harrison. *Who Was Charles Darwin?* New York: Grosset and Dunlap, 2005.

Jackson, M.H. *Galapagos: A Natural History*. East Lansing: Michigan State University Press, 1994.

Lawson, K. *Darwin and Evolution for Kids: His Life and Ideas with 21 Activities*. Chicago: Chicago Review, 2003.

Sloan, C., M. Leakey, and L. Leakey. *The Human Story: Our Evolution from Prehistoric Ancestors to Today*. New York: National Geographic Children's Books, 2004.

Swash, A., and R. Still. *Birds, Mammals, and Reptiles of the Galapagos Islands: An Identification Guide, 2nd Ed.* New Haven, Conn.: Yale University Press, 2001.

Web Sites

Evolution: A Journey into Where We're From and Where We're Going.
http://www.pbs.org/wgbh/evolution/

> *Here you can find a diversity of examples explaining fundamental principles of natural selection and evolution.*

The Society for the Study of Evolution.
http://www.evolutionsociety.org/
> *This Web site provides access to the premier international scientific society for the study of evolution.*

The TalkOrigins Archive: Exploring the Creation/Evolution Controversy.
http://www.talkorigins.org/
> *This site presents different perspectives on the creation-evolution topic.*

Understanding Evolution: Your One-Stop Source for Information on Evolution.
http://evolution.berkeley.edu/
> *Here you can find different resources and answers to all your questions about evolution and natural selection.*

Natural History of the Galápagos Islands.
http://www.rit.edu/~rhrsbi/GalapagosPages/NewGalapagos.html
> *This site provides information about the different plants and animals that live on the Galápagos Islands.*

The Complete Works of Charles Darwin.
http://www.darwin-literature.com/
> *This site contains electronic versions of the different books, manuscripts, and writings of Charles Darwin.*

Picture Credits

Index

About the Author

J. Phil Gibson holds degrees in botany from Oklahoma State University (B.S.) and the University of Georgia (M.S.) and in environmental population and organismic biology from the University of Colorado (Ph.D.). He is currently an associate professor in the Department of Botany and Microbiology and the Department of Zoology at the University of Oklahoma. His research investigates the ecology and evolution of plant reproductive systems. He also conducts conservation-focused research on plant species. He has published a variety of research papers and presented his work at scientific conferences. Gibson is a member of the Project Kaleidoscope Faculty for the 21st Century in recognition of his efforts to improve undergraduate science education. He is an active member of the Botanical Society of America.

Terri R. Gibson holds a degree in zoology from the University of Georgia (B.S.). She has worked as a scientific illustrator and also as a research assistant studying, among other things, plant evolution, plant population genetics, plant morphology, *E. coli*, and HIV. Currently, she is pursuing a career in children's literature.